THE WORLD ALMANAC

FOR KIDS

WORKBOOK

FIRST GRADE!

with activities by
Molly Smith, Lynn Brunelle,
and Christine Economos

chronicle books · san francisco

THIS BOOK BELONGS TO:

Typeset in Rockwell and Neutra.
ISBN 978-0-8118-7702-2

Manufactured by Toppan Leefung, Da Ling Shan Town, Dongguan, China in March 2012.
3 5 7 9 10 8 6 4 2

This product conforms to CPSIA 2008.

Chronicle Books LLC
680 Second Street
San Francisco, California 94107

www.chroniclekids.com

INTRODUCTION

Based on the No. 1 best-selling kids' almanac in the world, *The World Almanac for Kids* workbooks are chock-full of interesting facts, games, riddles, and brainteasers.

The activities in this workbook will help children practice the skills needed for success in first grade, covering all major areas—reading, writing, math, and science. While many other workbooks focus mainly on "skills and drills," this workbook also delves into engaging subjects like dinosaurs, weather, and transportation, so kids can learn new and exciting things while practicing important reading, writing, and math skills.

Exercises include finding rhyming words, solving riddles, adding coins, reading clocks, sequencing stories, identifying parts of animals and plants, matching dinosaurs to their names, and more.

Children may require an adult helper to read the directions. These workbooks can be a wonderful interactive activity for parents and children—and teachers and students—to do together. Enjoy!

- -

Molly Smith is an editor and writer of children's nonfiction, activity books, and games. She has also worked extensively with teachers and curriculum developers to create textbooks for the primary grades. She lives with her husband and daughters in Connecticut.

Lynne Brunelle is a former classroom teacher, a best-selling children's book author, and an Emmy Award–winning writer. Her educational projects range from the board game Cranium to the TV show *Bill Nye the Science Guy*. She is also the author of *Yoga for Chickens* and *Mama's Little Book of Tricks*, both available from Chronicle Books. She lives with her husband and two sons near Seattle.

Christine Economos is a writer and educator at the American Museum of Natural History in New York City. She is the author of *The World Almanac for Kids* Puzzler Deck *Dinosaur Science!* and *The World Almanac for Kids* Puzzler Deck *Ocean Science!* as well as other books for children.

TABLE OF CONTENTS

→Reading←

RHYMING RIDDLE

Can you circle the item that finishes this rhyming riddle?

Some are red.

Some are blue.

It's on your foot.

It's a _____.

RAINBOW RHYME

Can you find the object with a name that rhymes with each color? Draw a line to make each match.

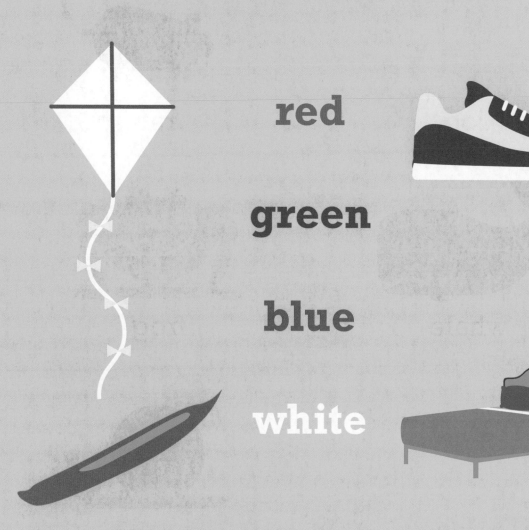

red

green

blue

white

RHYME TIME

Draw lines to match the animals that have rhyming names.

dog

rat

whale

frog

cat

snail

RHYME TIME II

Can you find a food that rhymes with each animal's name? Draw a line to make each match.

parrot   ape   snake

grape   cake   carrot

LINE UP

Coach Talia is picking players for the team.

Draw a line to match each player to the word that describes her.

tall   **taller**   **tallest**

CIRCUS CLAPS

Words can be divided into parts called **syllables**.

To find the syllables, clap as you speak the parts of each word.

tiger

clown

seal

acrobat

Circle the one who gets the most claps. Write the number here:

☐ claps

SARA'S SNACK

Sara only eats foods with two syllables.

Clap as you say each part of the words to count the syllables.

Circle the foods that Sara will eat.

spaghetti

apple

carrot

broccoli

milk

pretzel

TWO IN ONE

Can you find the two smaller words in each big word? Write them on the lines below each word.

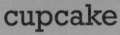

cupcake

football

mailbox

ladybug

RHYMING RIDDLE II

Can you circle the item that finishes this rhyming riddle?

It drives in mud.

It won't get stuck.

It's not a car.

It's a _____.

WHAT'S THE STORY?

Which words go best with the picture? Draw a line from the picture to the words that match.

1. Mac is a cat.
   He is in a hat.

2. Mac is a man.
   He has a hat.

SYLLABLES WITH SYLVIA

Sylvia's name has three syllables.

That means you clap three times when you say the parts of her name.

How many names with three syllables can you find below? Circle them.

elephant

tiger

bear

crocodile

monkey

kangaroo

MISSING MUSIC

These instruments are missing the first letters of their names. The letters are all at the bottom of the page. Write the missing letters in the blanks.

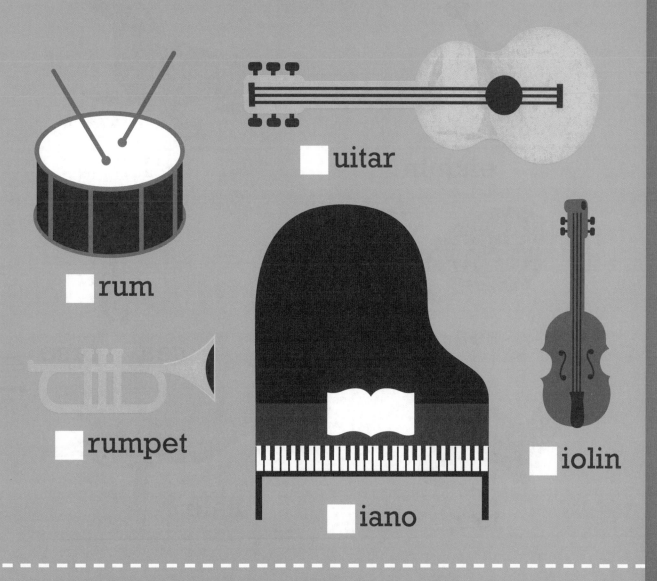

☐ uitar

☐ rum

☐ rumpet

☐ iano

☐ iolin

v   g   t   p   d

LOST LETTERS

Write in the missing letters to complete the name of each animal. You can find the letters at the bottom of the page.

☐ enguin

☐ eal

sea ☐ urtle

sea ☐ orse

☐ tter

☐ hale

o h w p s t

CREATURE FEATURE

Each of these sea animals has something to say.

Can you draw a line to match each animal to its quote?

1. As I grow bigger, I have to find a new home.

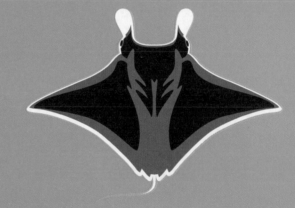

2. My webbed toes make me a good swimmer.

3. I may look dangerous, but I am harmless.

CHOPPED FRUIT

The names of these fruits have been chopped in two! Draw lines to match the parts.

le   ple

ap   mon

ch   apes

gr   erries

SYLLABLE SEA

Clap as you say each part of these animals' names. Each clap is a syllable.

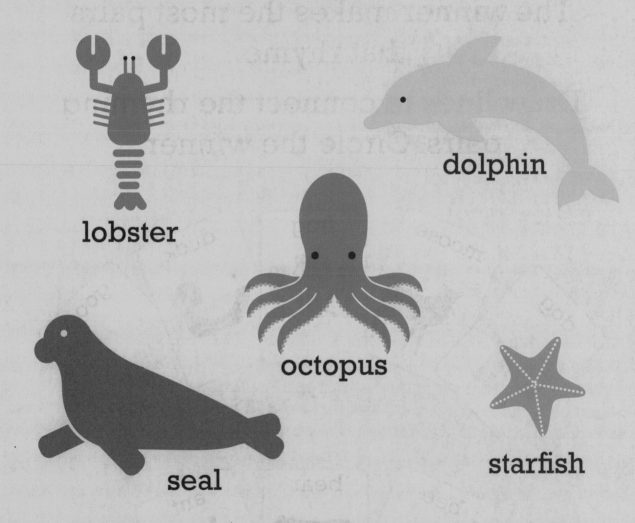

dolphin

lobster

octopus

seal

starfish

Which animal got the most claps? Circle it.

How many claps did it get?

☐ claps

LET'S PLAY CARDS!

Sam and Pam are playing a game. The winner makes the most pairs that rhyme.

Draw lines to connect the rhyming pairs. Circle the winner.

Pam's Cards

Sam's Cards

CLEAN UP

Claire is cleaning out her closet. She is organizing her things by the **first** letter of their names.

Draw lines to put each item in its box.

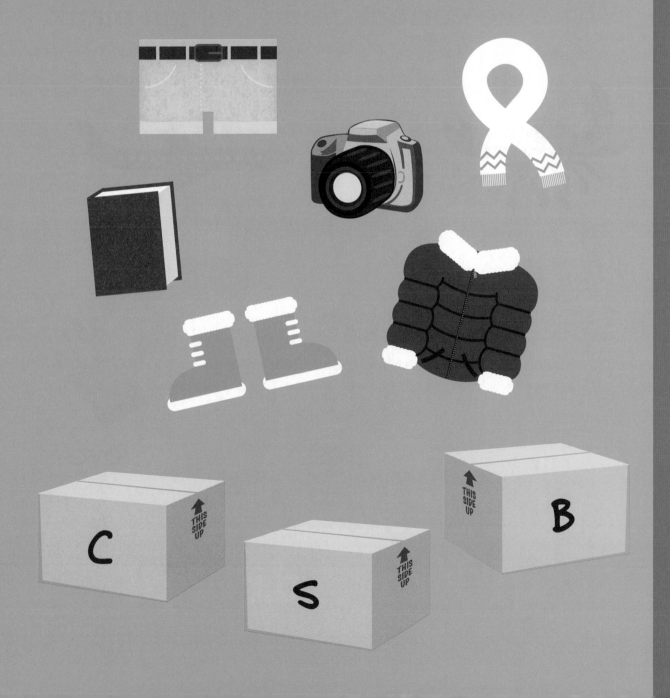

BLEND BUSTER

These words are missing their beginning blends.

Write the correct blend in each blank.

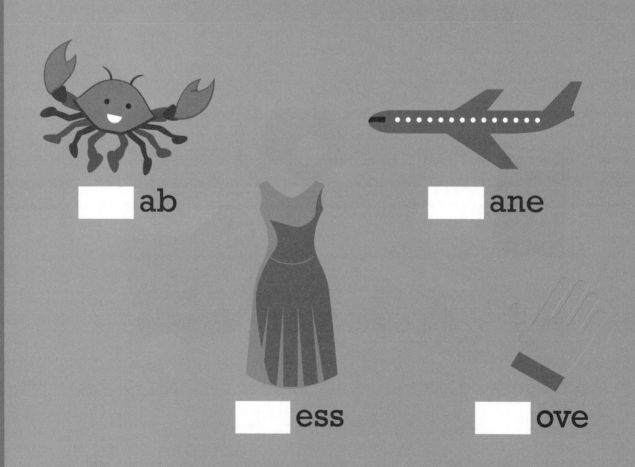

[ ] ab

[ ] ane

[ ] ess

[ ] ove

gl cr dr pl

LITTLE RIDDLE RHYMES

Can you pick the word that solves each riddle? Write the answer below each.

It is another word for ocean.

It sounds like

It makes a honking sound.

It sounds like

It gets you from here to there.

It sounds like

It is a good feeling.

It sounds like

goose proud sea train

CONTRACTION ACTION

A **contraction** is a short way of writing two words as one.

Read the words on each wheel.

Which contractions are made with the word in the center? Circle them.

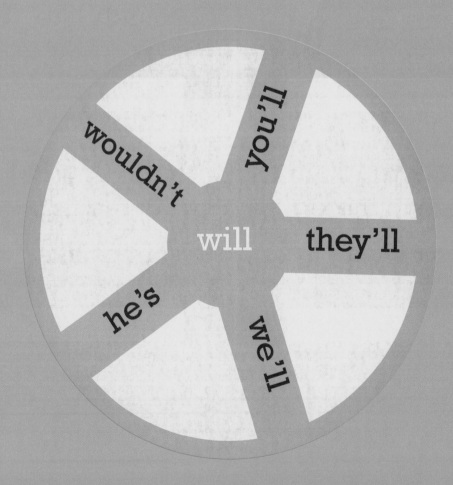

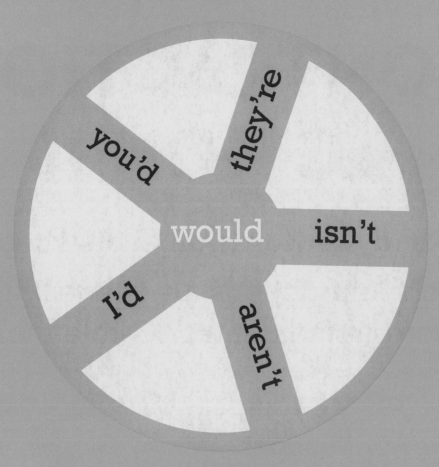

you'd · they're · would · isn't · I'd · aren't

I'm · you'll · are · they're · you're · he's

CONTRACTION ACTION II

Read the words on each wheel.
Which contractions are made with the
word in the center? Circle them.

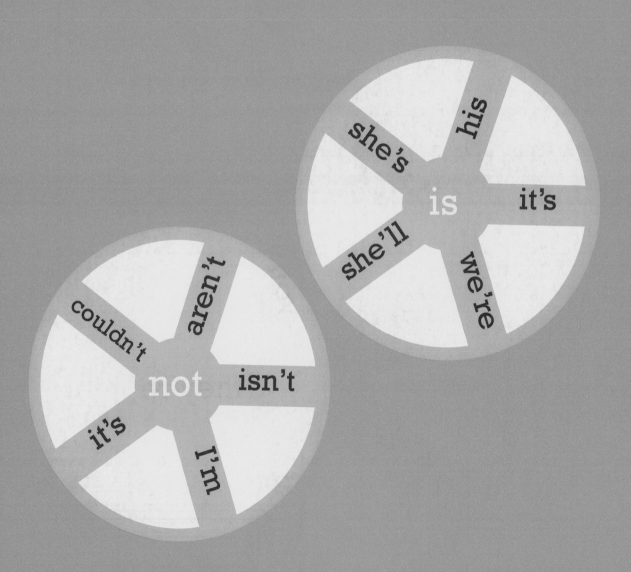

RUN THE BASES

The endings **-s**, **-ed**, and **-ing** are often added to the end of a **base** word.

Can you underline the base word on each base?

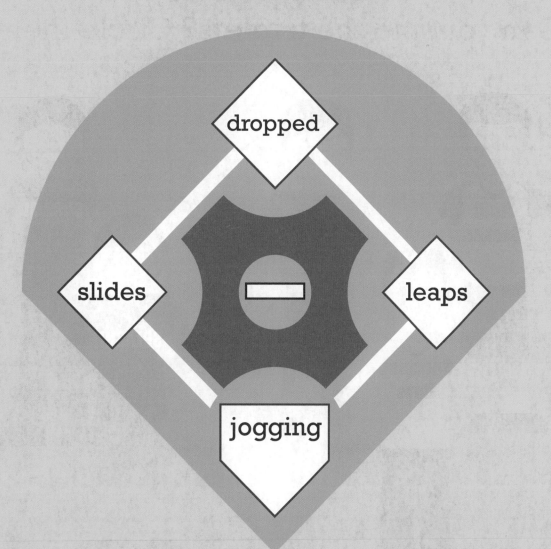

dropped

slides

leaps

jogging

Hint: Sometimes an extra letter is added before an ending. It is **not** part of the base word.

THREE IN A ROW

Trip, Skip, and Flip are triplets. Each triplet's shirt has a word that begins with **three consonants**.

Can you find the triplets? Circle them.

RUN THE BASES II

The endings **-s**, **-ed**, and **-ing** are often added to the end of a **base** word.

Can you underline the base word on each base?

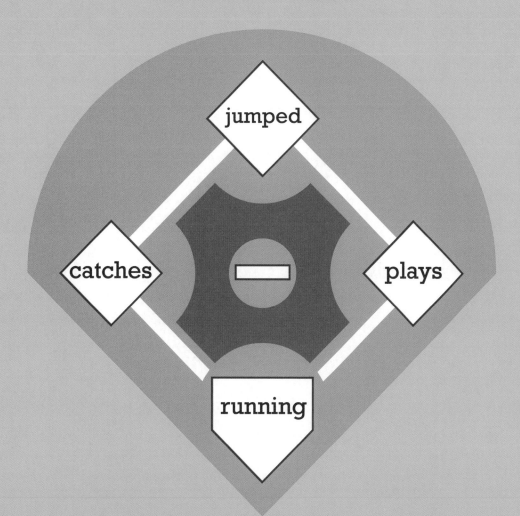

Hint: Sometimes an extra letter is added before an ending. It is **not** part of the base word.

RUN THE BASES III

The endings **-s**, **-ed**, and **-ing** are often added to the end of a **base** word.

Can you underline the base word on each base?

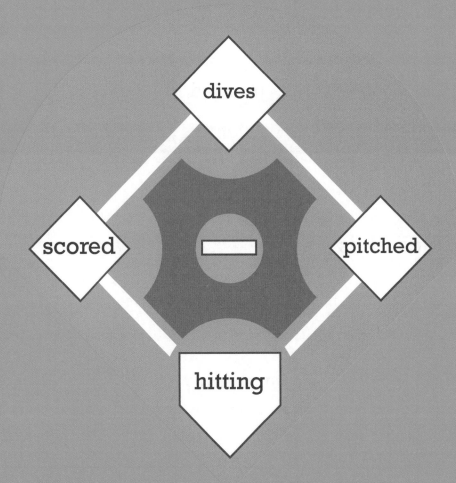

dives

scored

pitched

hitting

Hint: Sometimes an extra letter is added before an ending. It is **not** part of the base word.

FRUIT BOWL

Draw a line to match each fruit to the letter it begins with.

B

P

A

C

G

ANIMAL JUMBLE

Farmer Ann is trying to separate her animals from Farmer Bob's animals.

All of Ann's animals begin with **A**.

All of Bob's animals begin with **B**.

Draw lines to match each animal to the first letter of its name.

RHYME TIME III

Draw a star ⭐ by the vehicle that rhymes with **star**. Draw a raindrop 💧 next to the vehicle that rhymes with **rain**.

SOUNDS LIKE...

Two of these objects have names that sound the same. Draw a line between the two objects whose names sound the same.

FLOUR

WHICH DOES NOT BELONG?

The words in each boat below are supposed to be alike in some way. Which word does not belong in each boat? Circle it.

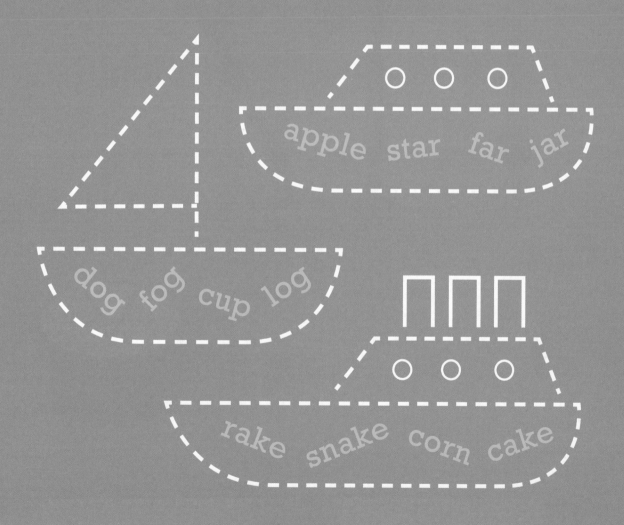

apple star far jar

dog fog cup log

rake snake corn cake

TUNE TIME

Which three instruments have strings?
Write their names below.

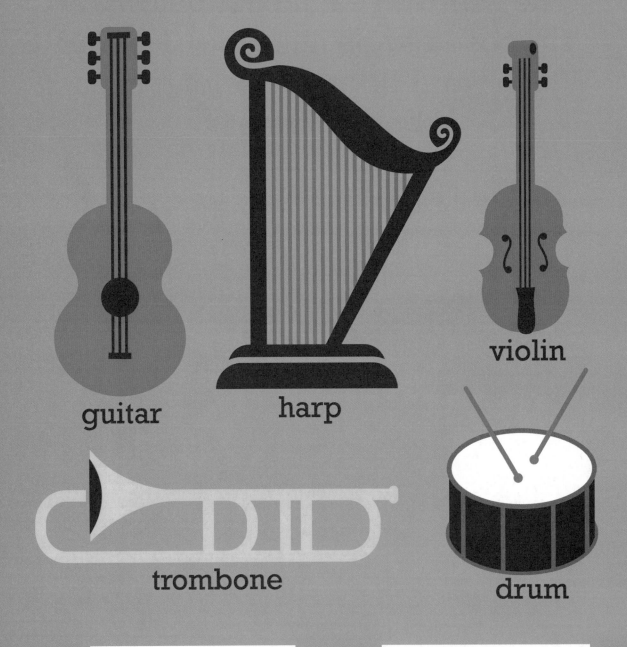

guitar   harp

violin

trombone   drum

1. _____   2. _____

3. _____

RHYME TIME IV

Each list includes three rhyming words and one extra word that does not rhyme. Write the extra words in the blank spaces to find a secret message!

on	ton	farm
dawn	tune	fun
fawn	soon	arm
one	moon	charm

Rhyming is _____

_____ of _____ .

ART MUSEUM RHYME TIME

Which of the things shown rhyme with **blue**? Circle them.

BARNYARD RHYME TIME

Can you find the animals with names that rhyme with **fog**? Write their names below.

donkey

dog

duck

frog

sheep

1. [   ]   2. [   ]

A DIFFERENT TUNE

Which instrument does not belong?
Write its name below.

drum

French horn

trumpet

trombone

tuba

GET AROUND WITH NOUNS

A **noun** is a word for a person, place, or thing. Can you find the nouns below? Circle them.

snowman

slowly   pizza

shoe   eat

funny   train

umbrella

ACTION!

A **verb** is an action word that tells
what a person, place, or thing does.
There are four verbs in the list below.
Can you circle them?

climb

sandbox

run

bucket

chalk

hop

jump

pants

ABC CATS

These cat names are out of order. Write them in A-B-C order in the blanks below.

lion

cheetah

tiger

puma

jaguar

FINISH YOUR FOOD

Each food is missing a letter. Use your letter stickers to fill in the blanks.

izza

ake

andwhich

ookie

atermelon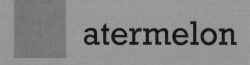

ANIMAL ADVENTURES

These animals need a ride back to the zoo.

Which animal's name rhymes with each thing that goes? Draw a line to make each match.

goat

truck

sheep

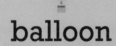

balloon

raccoon

jeep

duck

boat

TALK ABOUT TRAINS

Which word describes each train? Write the word in the blank below each train.

big   **long**   **short**

→Phonics←

STUCK IN THE MIDDLE

Missy always gets stuck in the middle of words.

Can you help her find each missing letter? Write one in each blank.

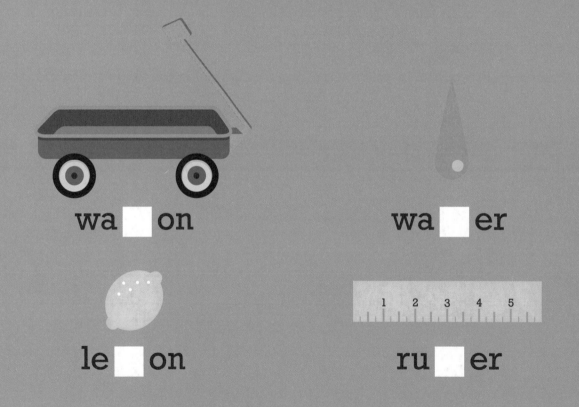

wa ▢ on

wa ▢ er

le ▢ on

ru ▢ er

l   m   g   t

VINCE'S VOWELS

Vince is trying to fix these words. Which vowel does he need to make each word whole again? Write it in the blank.

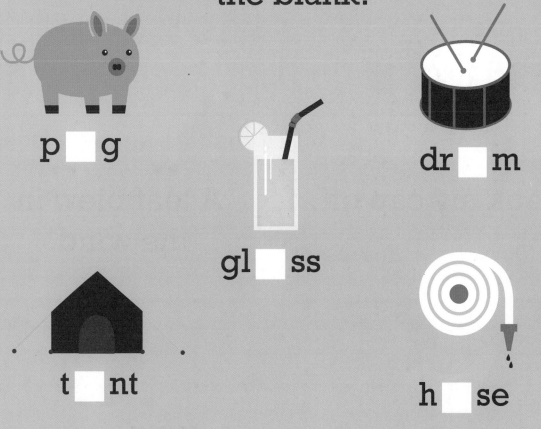

p　g

gl　ss

dr　m

t　nt

h　se

a　e　i　o　u

MIDDLE MATCH

Say the name of each animal. Then read the sentence below it.

Which word in the sentence has the same **middle** sound as the animal's name? Circle it.

I took my cap off.

A leaf blew in the wind.

We made mud pies in the yard.

I slid down the wet slide.

WE ARE FAMILY

Word families share letter patterns and sounds.

Can you draw a line to put each word in the right family home?

still

will

mall

well

bell

fill

ball

fell

stall

The **-ill** Family

The **-all** Family

The **-ell** Family

MAY DAY

Jay made up a poem about his favorite month: May.

Can you find all the words that have the long **a** sound, as in **May**? Circle them.

May Day
You can enjoy May
in so many ways.
You can sail on the lake
on warm, windy days.

You can walk in the rain
and make up a game.
Or stay in your house
and play games just the same!

CAN YOU C?

Carl likes **c** words that begin with the **k** sound, as in his name.

Celia likes **c** words that begin with the **s** sound, as in her name.

Draw a line to match each word to the person who likes it.

circle   celery   carrot

Carl   Celia

crayon

city

WE ARE FAMILY II

Word families share letter patterns and sounds. Draw lines to put each word in the correct family home.

nest

boat

best

meat

coat

goat

seat

vest

beat

The -o mily

The -eat Family

The -est Family

I SPY!

Mike likes to play I Spy. He spies only words that have the long **i** sound, as in his name.

Write the answer to each of Mike's clues in the blank below it.

I spy something you ride.

I spy something my dad wears to work.

I spy a number.

I spy a place where bees live.

hive   **train**   **bike**   **tie**
nine   **six**   **hill**   **suit**

QUICK CHANGE

These words are changing letters!
Then they become new words.

Which picture solves each problem?
Draw a line to make each match.

The first one has been done for you.

hat   Change **h** to **b** =

cap   Change **p** to **t** = **?**

top   Change **t** to **m** = **?**

clap   Change **a** to **i** = **?**

ball   Change **a** to **e** = **?**

STIR IT UP

Vern is making soup.

Which pots only have words that have the same **r-controlled** sound as Vern's name? Circle them.

storm
clerk

whir
hurt

bird
turn
her

sir
deer
fur

JUNE TUNE

June made up a song about her favorite month: June!

Can you find all the words that have the long **u** sound, as in **June**? Circle them.

June

It has clear blue skies,
fresh fruits and juice.
It has bright tie-dyes
and cute bathing suits.

It has barbecues
and sandy dunes.
It has happy tunes—
and it's called June!

DROP A LETTER

These words are dropping letters!
Then they become new words.

Which picture solves each problem?
Draw a line to make each match.

The first one has been done for you.

scar − **s** = **?**

chat − **c** = **?**

pant − **p** = **?**

snail − **s** = **?**

train − **t** = **?**

CLUSTER BUSTER

Sly is a sneak! He has swiped the **s clusters** from the beginnings of these words.

Write the correct blend in each blank.

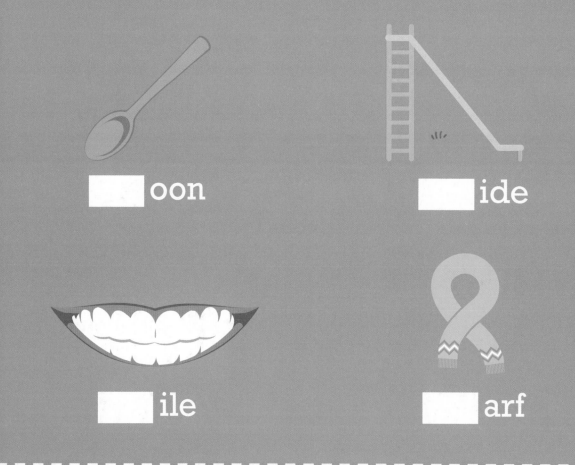

⬜oon

⬜ide

⬜ile

⬜arf

sp   sc   sl   sm

ZANY ZOO

Jack and Judd care for animals whose names have a **short** vowel sound, like their names.

Jake and Julie care for animals whose names have a **long** vowel sound, like their names.

Draw lines to put each animal with the correct zookeepers.

duck

ape

skunk

| Jack + Judd | Jake + Julie |

ox

mule

WATCH OUT!

The letters **ow** can make the sound **ow**, as in **cow**, or the long **o** sound, as in **slow**.

This cow wants to get back to the barn.

Which path only has words that make the same sound as **cow**?
Draw the path.

START

how	town	grow
throw	down	mow
yellow	frown	follow
crow	gown	tow

FINISH

B QUIET

In some words, the letter **b** is silent.

Can you find the words in which **b** does not make a sound? Circle them.

thumb

lamb

cube

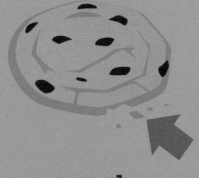

crumb

comb

cob

END BLENDS

The blends have fallen off the ends of these words!

Write the correct blend in each blank.

te [ ]

sta [ ]

ma [ ]

tru [ ]

si [ ]

li [ ]

nk
nt

mp
sk

ng
st

O.K. CORRAL

These **k** words are on the loose. In some of the words, the letter **k** is silent.

Can you round up the words in which **k** does not make a sound? Draw a line from each silent-k word to the lasso.

king

kite

kitten

knob

knot

key

knife

knit

knight

ADD A LETTER

These words are adding letters in order to become new words!

Which picture solves each problem? Draw a line to make each match.

The first one has been done for you.

g + love =

c + lock = ?

w + heel = ?

pl + ant = ?

sp + ring = ?

JUNGLE JIM

Jim loves to climb the jungle gym. But he will only hold onto bars with words that make the **j** sound, as in his name.

Draw Jim's path to the top. He can move up, across and diagonally.

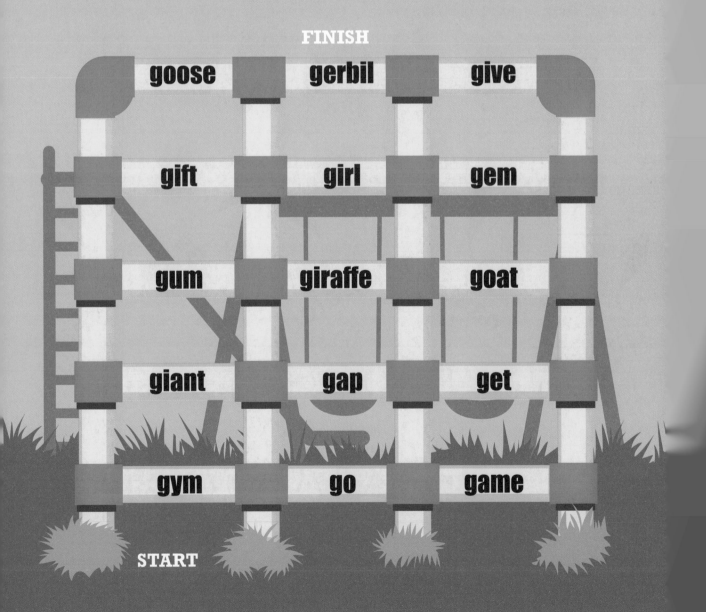

FINISH

goose	gerbil	give
gift	girl	gem
gum	giraffe	goat
giant	gap	get
gym	go	game

START

SHARK BAIT

Sharif is fishing for sharks.

The sharks in these parts only bite lures with **sh** on them.

Which lures will the Shark bite? Circle them.

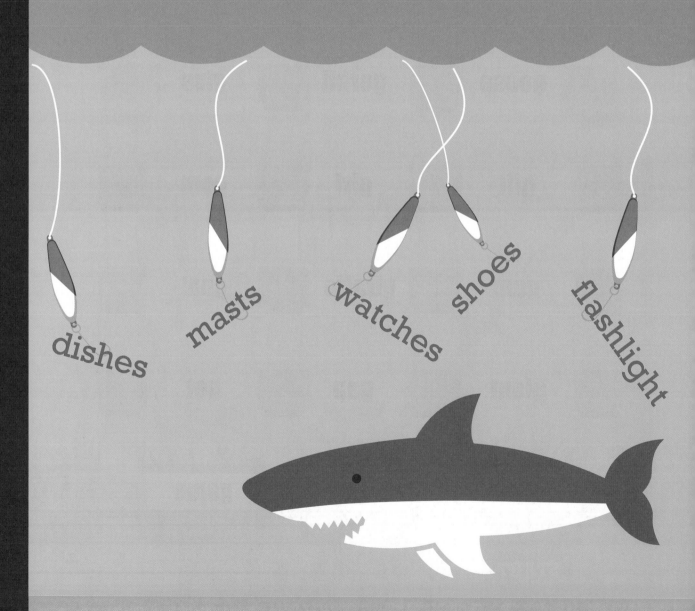

dishes

masts

watches

shoes

flashlight

DOUBLE STUFF

Say the name of each picture.
Each name has double letters
in the middle.

Can you draw a line to match each
picture to its double letters?

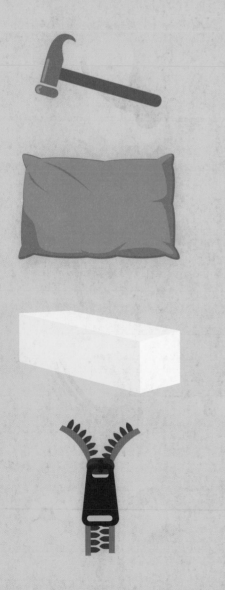

ll

mm

pp

tt

SO SWEET

Swifty is good at lots of sports. But his best sport begins with the letters **sw**.

Which sport is Swifty's sweetest? Write **SW** below it.

LOOK FOR A CROOK

The police are looking for a crook. The crook left a trail of words with the same **o** sound as **crook**.

Draw the path that leads to the crook.

START

cook	stood	toot
tooth	shook	hoop
soon	wood	book
zoom	snoop	foot

FINISH

READY OAR NOT

Corey and Tory are going to row across the pond. They need to choose the two oars that have only words with the **or** sound.

Which oars do they need?
Color them brown.

more   your   boar   care

core   soar   floor   cord

door   roar   horse   for

four   her   bored   port

WHAT AM I?

Can you solve each riddle?

Each word is missing a pair of consonants. Use **letter stickers** to fill in the missing letters.

I am red.

I am a fruit.

I am a ⬛⬛erry.

I live in the sea.

I am not a fish.

I am a ⬛⬛ale.

I can open a door.

I turn left and right.

I am a ⬛⬛ob.

IT'S E-Z

Can you find the picture that shows what each word will turn into when you add a final **e**? Draw a line to make each match.

kit

tap

cub

cap

D-DAY

The animals are loose! Farmer Dan from The Dandy Dude Ranch is trying to collect his animals. Put a **D sticker** on all the animals that begin with **D**.

STUCK ON VOWELS

These vehicles are stuck without their vowels. Add **letter stickers** to fill in the missing vowels.

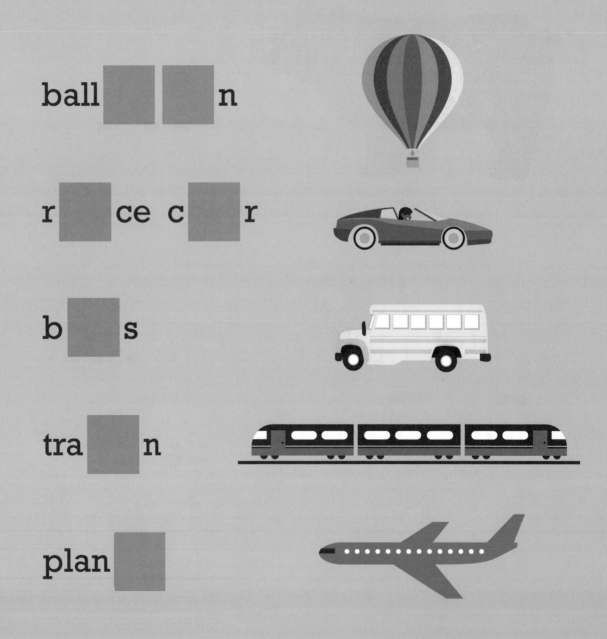

ball⬜⬜n

r⬜ce c⬜r

b⬜s

tra⬜n

plan⬜

Vocabulary

WORD PARTY

A **noun** is a person, place, or thing. A **verb** is a word that tells what a person or thing does. Write an **N** next to all the nouns in this word party. Write a **V** next to the verbs.

gift

blow

cake

eat

hat

BETTER TOGETHER!

Think of the word for each picture.

Can you put the words together to make new words? Write the new word in each blank.

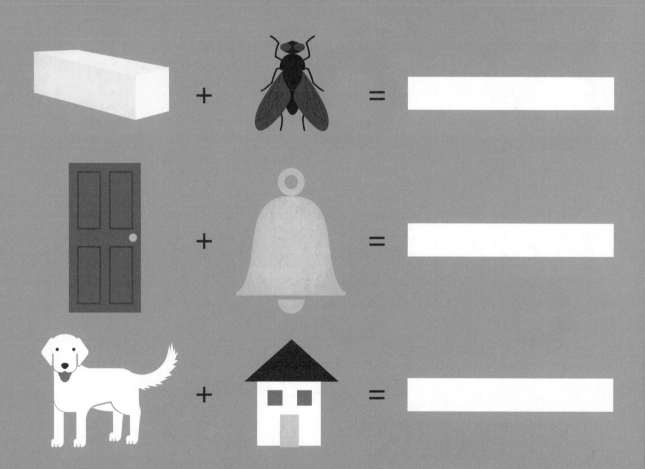

doorbell   butterfly   doghouse

BIG WHEELS

Travis saw some big wheels
at the truck show.

Draw a line to match each word with
the truck it describes.

bigger

big

biggest

MOODY TRUDY

Trudy is making faces in her mirror. Can you draw a line to match each face to the right word?

mad   **sad**   **surprised**   **happy**

FISH PARTS

Pete drew a fish, but he can't remember its parts.

Can you help him label his fish? Write a word on each line.

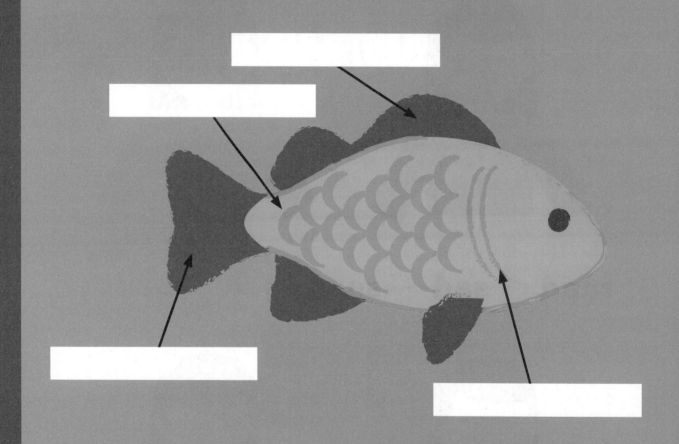

tail   **fin**

gill   **scales**

RABBITS ON THE RUN

These rabbits are running wild!
Draw a line to match each path to the word that describes it.

 **curved**

 **zigzag**

 **straight**

TWO FOR ONE

A **compound** word is made up of two smaller words.

butter   fly

Find the small words in each compound word. Where can you cut each word into two? Draw a line to make the cut.

cupcake   bedroom

popcorn   wishbone

doorbell   mailbox

TAKE TWO

Say the name of each picture.

Then find the two words that join to make its name. Write the word below each picture.

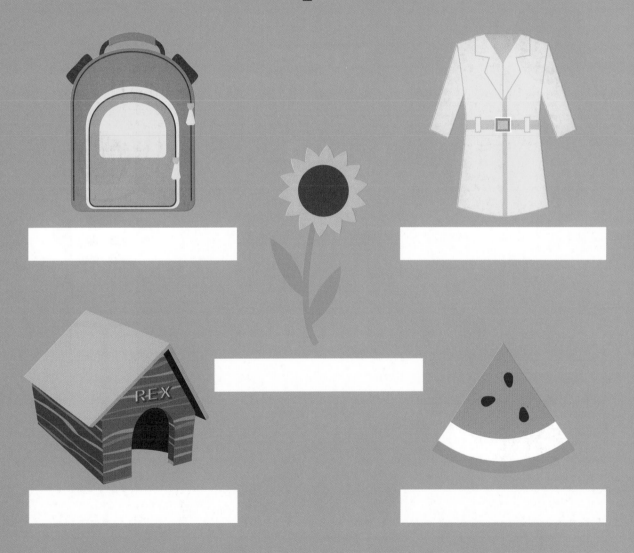

back   dog   coat   flower   house

melon   pack   rain   sun   water

SPACE RACE!

Can you draw a line to match each picture to the correct space-themed word?

 moon

 sun

 star

 Earth

 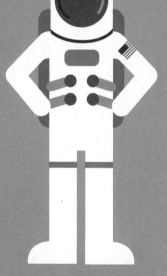

 rocket

 astronaut

WHERE IS BONGO?

Match each picture to the word that tells where Bongo is hiding.

outside

under

inside

over

INVENTIONS

Draw a line to match each invention to its name.

train   zipper   plane   pen   phone

WATER, WATER EVERYWHERE

Which of these words does *not* name a body of water? Circle it.

ocean   sea

island

lake   pond

BONGO'S FEELINGS

Bongo is on the loose in the classroom! Can you pick the correct word to tell how Bongo is feeling in each picture? Write the word in the blank below the picture.

happy   bored   scared   sad

WHAT DO I WEAR?

Hazel is the most fashionable kid on the block, but she sometimes doesn't know the names of her clothes! Help her by matching each item to its name.

mittens

flip-flops

sun hat

T-shirt

swimsuit

parka

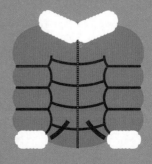

ski cap

HAPPY TRUDY

An **adjective** is a word that describes something or someone. Circle the adjectives that say something **nice** about Trudy.

grumpy   messy

smart   friendly

sweet   rude

mean   kind

→ Math Skills ←

VEGGIE VOTE

Miss Molly's class made a chart.

Each kid said which veggie he or she likes best.

Circle the veggie the class likes the **least**. How many votes did that veggie get? Write the number below.

☐ votes

Favorite Vegetables

FISHY FIGURES

Kenzo's class made a tally chart of favorite fish. A tally chart uses lines to show how many items are counted.

| stands for 1. ||||| stands for 5.

Circle the fish that got the **most** votes. How many votes did it get? Write the number below.

☐ votes

Fish	Votes
Clown fish	||||| ||
Jellyfish	|||
Shark	|||||

WHAT'S THE NUMBER?

Which number is one hundred three?
Draw a circle ◯ around it.

Which number is three hundred one?
Draw a rectangle ▭ around it.

130

1003

301

103

SPENDY SUZY

Spendy Suzy bought the **most** expensive bike from her choices below. Write an **S** next to Suzy's bike.

Suzy's friend Carrie bought the **least** expensive bike. Write a **C** next to Carrie's bike.

$15.00

$100.00

$99.00

$25.00

TREASURE CHEST

Priscilla the pirate found three treasure chests. Which one contains the **most** money? Circle it.

HOW MUCH?

Which group of coins is worth more?
Circle it.

10¢

10¢

This group is worth ⬚ cents.

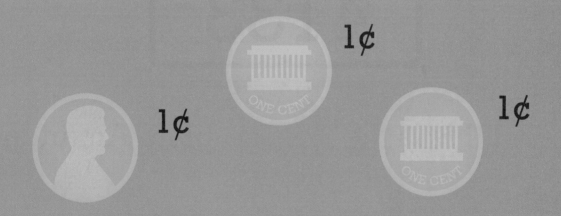

1¢

1¢

1¢

This group is worth ⬚ cents.

LICENSE PLATES

Alex and Amanda are playing a game on a family trip. The person who finds the highest number on a license plate wins.

This is the license plate Alex picked:

And this is the license plate Amanda picked:

Circle the winner.

Now circle the winner of this round:

Alex picked:

MARYLAND
2018

Amanda picked:

INDIANA
3009

Last round! Who won?

Alex picked:

UTAH
4991

Amanda picked:

MONTANA
4892

SPENDY SUZY II

Spendy Suzy is shopping for chairs. She decides to buy the **most** expensive one. Write an **S** next to Suzy's chair.

Suzy's friend Carrie bought the **least** expensive chair. Write a **C** next to Carrie's chair.

$147.99

$450.00

$200.00

$45.00

SQUARE SEARCH

How many squares do you see below?
Make a check mark ✓ inside each one.
Write the number here:

TRI TRI AGAIN

How many triangles do you see below?
Make a check mark inside each one.
Write the number here:

WHAT'S THE NUMBER? II

Which number is thirty-three?
Make a circle ◯ around it.

Which number is three hundred
thirty-three? Make a box ☐ around it.

30

333

33

3

QUACK ATTACK!

Draw a line to split the ducks in each box into two equal groups.

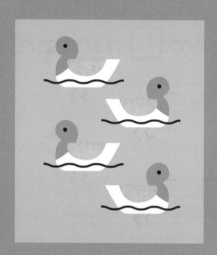

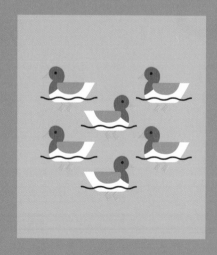

HOW MUCH? II

Circle the amount that is worth more.

 25¢    25¢

 25¢   25¢    25¢

TALLY HO!

Mike's class made a tally chart to show their favorite ocean animals. Use the tally chart to answer the questions.

- How many children chose the dolphin?

- Which animal got the **fewest** votes?

- Which animals got the **same** amount of votes?

dolphin		卌			
shark						
seal		卌		
crab		卌		

MISSING PIECE

Kai put together his jigsaw puzzle, but there's one piece missing. Which is it?

Draw a line from the missing piece to the empty spot.

STUCK ON COINS!

Add **coin stickers** in the blanks so each group will add up to the amount shown.

5¢ + = 7¢

5¢ + = 10¢

25¢ + = 28¢

10¢   10¢   +   = 21¢

5¢   5¢   +   = 15¢

1¢   5¢   +   = 11¢

1¢   10¢   +   = 12¢

GREATER GROUPS

Count the things that go in each group.

Which group is **greater** than the other? Write this symbol **>** with the open part facing the **greater** group.

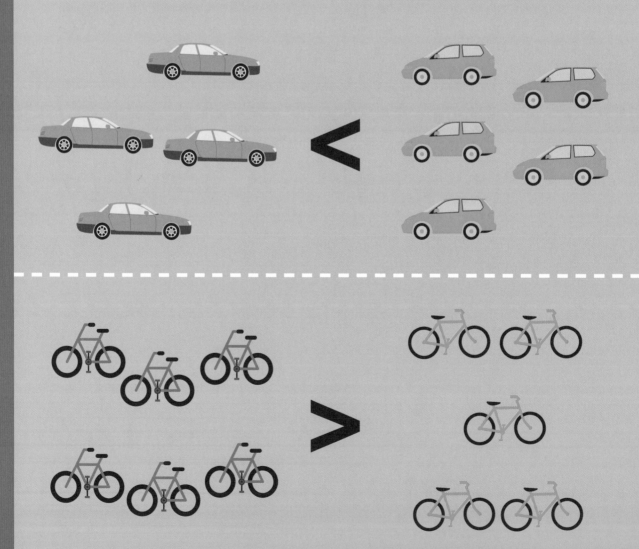

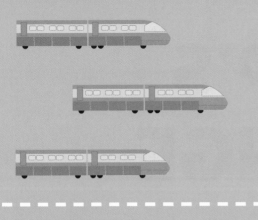

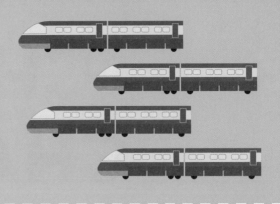

CHIP'S CHANGE

Chip has a pocket full of spare change. Can you help him put his coins in order from the smallest value to the largest?

Draw a line to show his path.

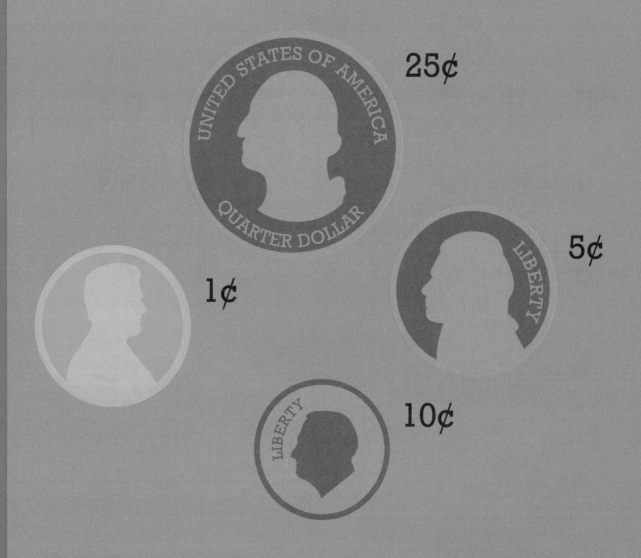

25¢

1¢

5¢

10¢

OFF TO SCHOOL

Mr. Mack's class made a chart to show how they get to school. Use the chart to answer the questions.

- How many students ride a bus?
- How many students ride a bike?
- How do most students get to school?

How We Travel to School					
car	★	★	★		
bus	★	★	★	★	
bike	★	★			
walk	★	★	★	★	★

GREATER GROUPS II

Count the dinosaurs in each group.

Which group is **greater** than the other? Write this symbol **>** with the open part facing the **greater** group.

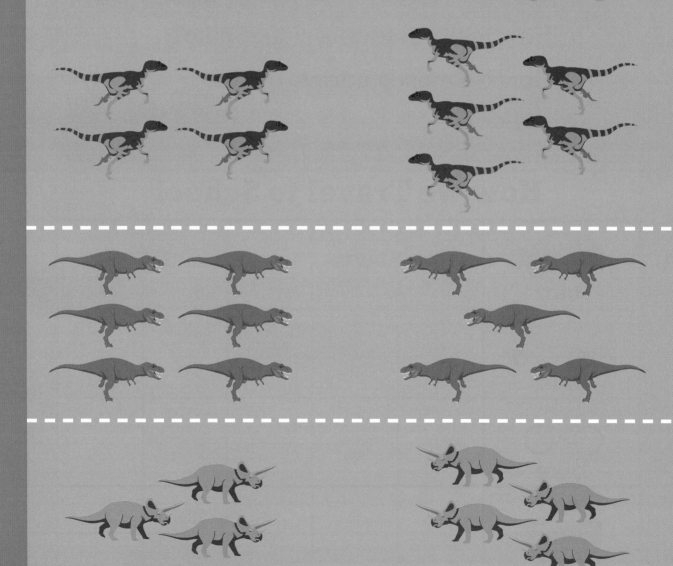

→ **Addition** ←
and
Subtraction

ONE MORE!

Max always wants one more!

Count the toys in each group.

Then draw a line to match it to the number that would be one more.

3

4

6

EVEN STEVEN

Steven wants to make his
scale balance.

That means it must have the same
amount of weight on both sides.

Draw in the number of weights that
will make the scale balance.

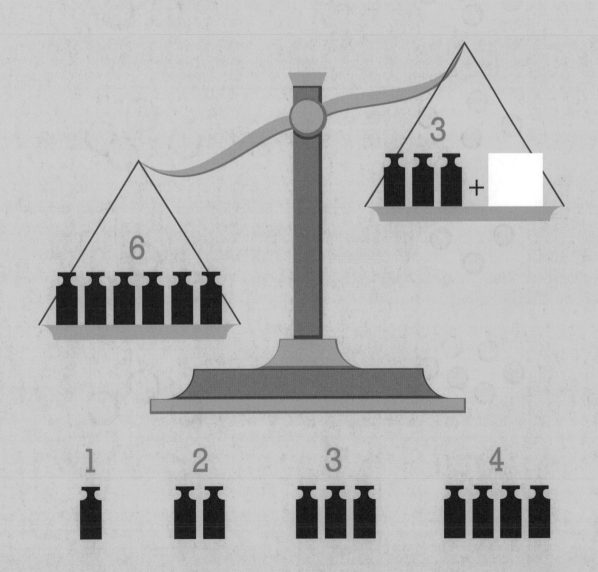

BERRY PICKING

All the muffins need to have
eight cranberries.

Draw a line to each muffin to the
amount of cranberries it still needs.

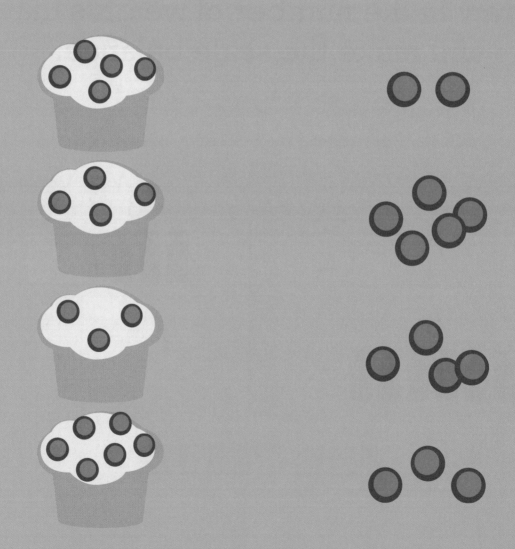

CUPCAKE COUNTERS

Marv made **four** cupcakes.

Min made **six** cupcakes.

How many cupcakes did they make in all?

Circle the picture that shows the right answer.

COOKIE COOKS

Ted and Ned made **ten** cookies.

Each boy ate **one** cookie.

How many cookies are left?

Circle the picture that shows
the right answer.

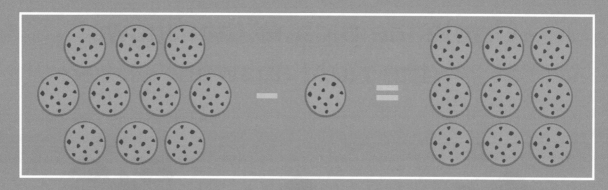

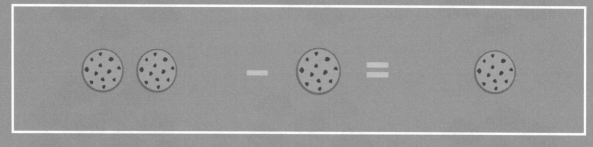

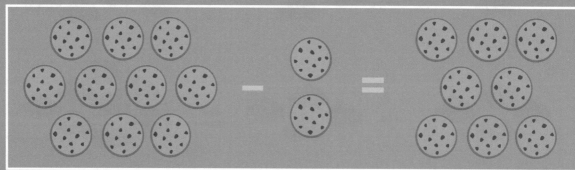

EVEN STEVEN II

Steven wants to make his
scale balance.

That means it must have the same
amount of weight on both sides.

Which two numbers will make the
scale balance? Draw in the number
of weights in the blanks.

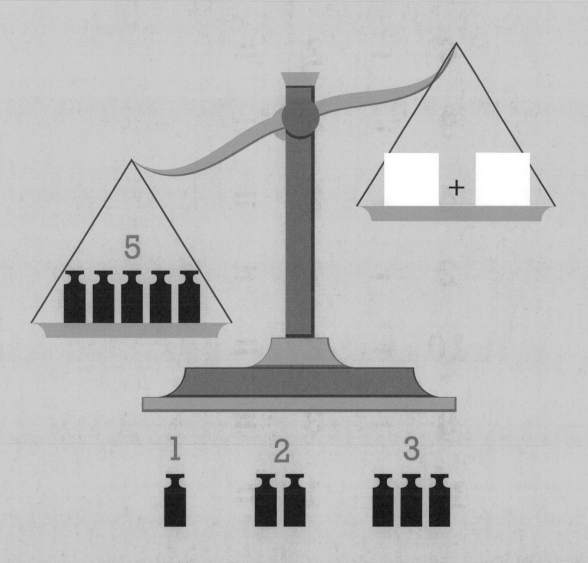

ONE TO NINE

Use your **number stickers** to fill in the answer for each number sentence. Each number from one to nine appears once.

10 − 3 =

8 − 5 =

6 − 2 =

9 − 4 =

4 − 2 =

2 − 1 =

10 − 2 =

9 − 3 =

10 − 1 =

PIZZA PARTY

Peyton loves pizza and he's having a party! His mom, dad, and two sisters are invited.

How many people will be at the party including Peyton? ▪

Which pizza is cut to serve each person **two slices**? Circle it.

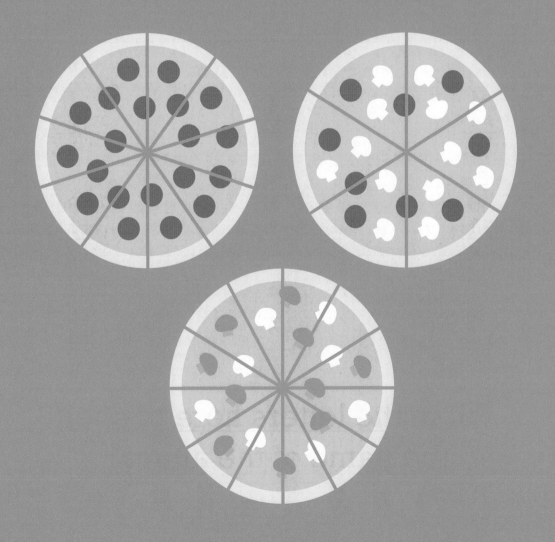

PARTY ANIMAL

All the animals were invited to play party games, except one. Solve each problem to find out who was left out. The letters above all the even number answers will spell the name of the animal.

C
5
+1

M
4
-1

H
6
+2

E
4
+4

L
9
-6

O
7
+2

E
6
-4

T
8
-4

S
6
+1

A
10
- 2

L
4
+3

H
6
+4

Fill in the letters here to spell the name of the animal.

■ ■ ■ ■ ■ ■

COOKIE COOKS II

Ruby and Maya made **eight** cookies.

Each girl ate **two** cookies.

How many cookies are left?

Circle the picture that shows the right answer.

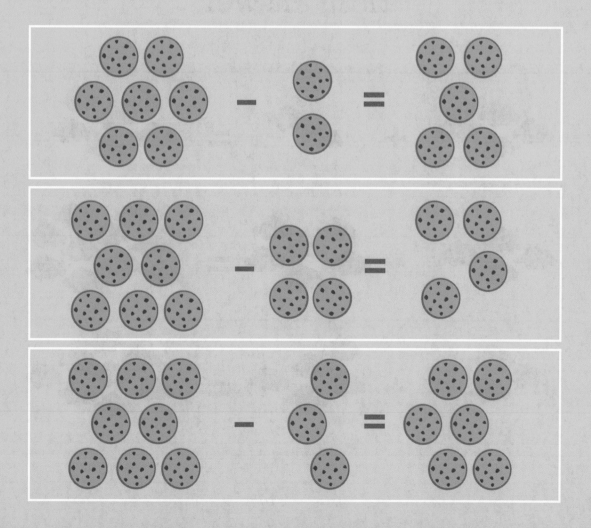

CUPCAKE COUNTERS II

Hannah made **three** cupcakes.

Julia made **five** cupcakes.

How many cupcakes did they make in all?

Circle the picture that shows the right answer.

NUMBER JUMBLE

Molly's math homework is mixed up. Draw a line to connect each picture to its number sentence.

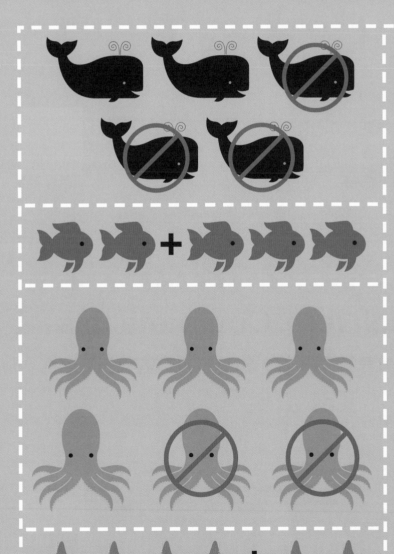

$$6 - 2 = 4$$

$$2 + 3 = 5$$

$$4 + 2 = 6$$

$$5 - 3 = 2$$

FRUITY FRAN

Fruity Fran ate three pineapples, two mangoes, and three bananas.

How many pieces of fruit did she eat in all? Complete the number sentence.

Kai ate much less. Complete this number sentence to see how much Kai ate.

→ Shapes ←
and
Measurements

CHART YOUR SHAPES

Fill this chart with pictures of each shape and **number stickers**.

Name of shape	Picture of shape	Number of sides
triangle		
square		
diamond		

Name of shape	Picture of shape	Number of sides
rectangle		
trapezoid		
pentagon		
hexagon		
octagon		

TALENTED TRIANGLES

When triangles get together, they can make all sorts of shapes. See what you can make with your **triangle stickers**.

Can you make a square out of **2** triangles?

Can you make a rectangle out of **4** triangles?

Can you make a trapezoid out of **3** triangles?

Can you make a hexagon out of **6** triangles?

What else can you create with your shape stickers? Use this space to make something!

BIG BUGS

Before the dinosaurs roamed, insects were huge! Some of their relatives are alive today.

Can you draw a line to match each insect to its size?

Hint: Compare the sizes of the pictures.

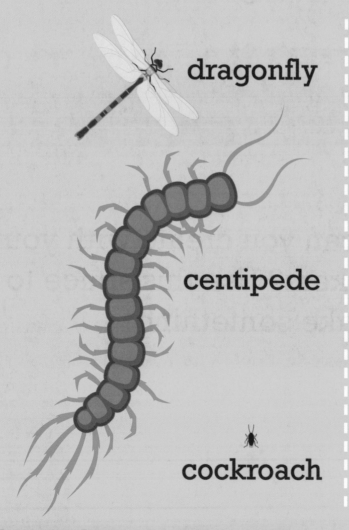

dragonfly

3½ inches

centipede

2½ feet

cockroach

20 feet

Insects shown roughly to scale.

READY FOR TAKEOFF!

Quetzalcoatlus was a flying reptile.

Which of these flyers has the same wingspan as Quetzalcoatlus? Circle it.

Hint: A wingspan is the distance from one wing tip to the other.

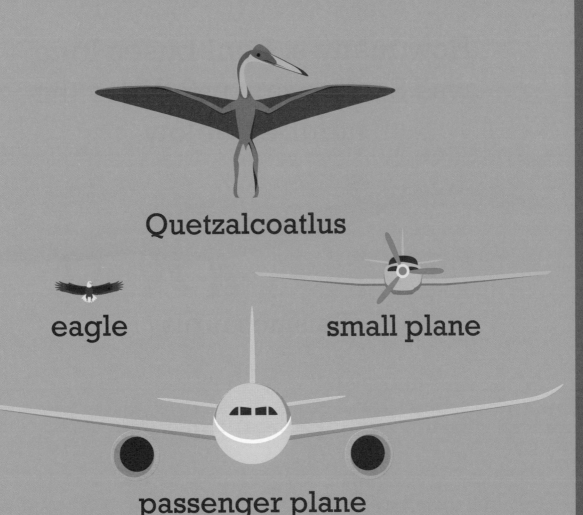

Quetzalcoatlus

eagle

small plane

passenger plane

SIZE ME UP

Spinosaurus was **one** school bus long.

Spinosaurus

How many school buses long
was Seismosaurus? Write the
number below.

Seismosaurus

school buses

TALL TALE

Which dinosaur was about 10 feet tall? Write **10** below it.

Which dinosaur was about 20 feet tall? Write **20** below it.

Which dinosaur was about 50 feet tall? Write **50** below it.

10 FT

Anatotitan   Brachiosaurus   Tyrannosaurus

HEAVY WEIGHTS

Compare these dinosaurs.
Can you draw a line to match each dinosaur to its weight?

6 tons

12 tons

80 tons

Dinosaurs not shown exactly to scale.

WHO'S THE SHRIMP?

Which of these shrimp is about
3 inches long? Circle it.

 pink shrimp

 tiger shrimp

 krill

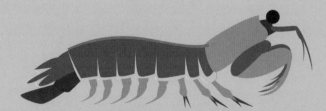 peacock shrimp

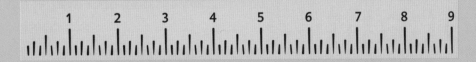

How long is the longest shrimp?
It is ⬜ inches long.

ORDER UP

Can you arrange these animals in order from smallest to largest? Write the correct order on the right. Start with the smallest on top.

cat

mouse

horse

whale

bee

elephant

HEAVY HITTER

Write **1**, **2**, **3**, **4**, or **5** next to each animal to put them in order from lightest to heaviest. Start with **1** for the lightest.

REPORT FOR DUTY!

It's up to you to give the weather report today!

Which thermometer shows the temperature for each picture? Draw a line to make each match.

85°

60°

20°

MEASURE UP

Which snake measures 3 inches?
Draw a circle ◯ around it.

Which snake measures 4 inches?
Draw a box ☐ around it.

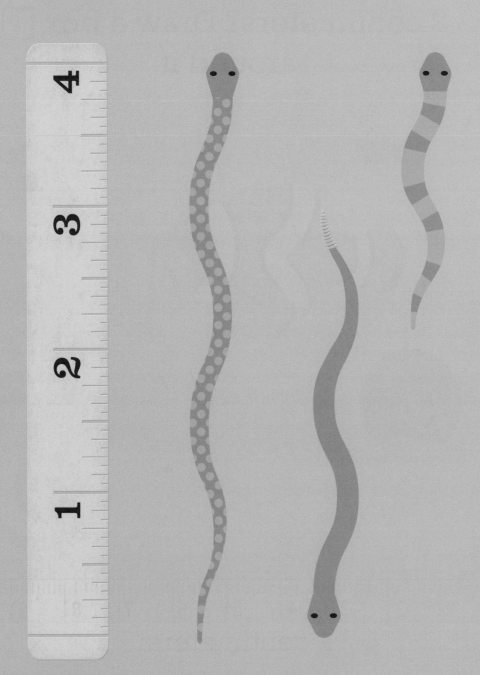

MEASURE UP II

Which animal measures 3.5 centimeters? Draw a circle ⭕ around it.

Which animal measures 2 centimeters? Draw a box ☐ around it.

IT'S RAINING, IT'S POURING

Walter the weatherman always records the rainfall.

Draw a circle ◯ around the day it rained the **most**.

Draw a box ☐ around the day it rained the **least**.

Monday   Tuesday   Wednesday

Thursday   Friday

HOT STUFF!

Hal lives in the desert where it can get really hot.

He records the temperature every day.

Write an **H** below the hottest day.
Write a **C** below the coolest day

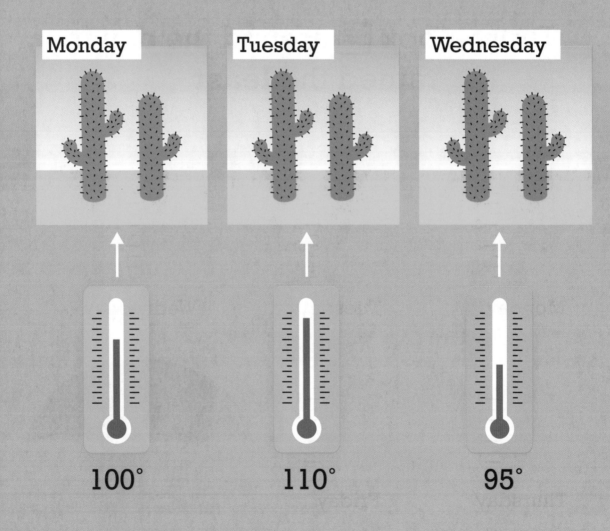

| Monday | Tuesday | Wednesday |
| 100° | 110° | 95° |

→ Clocks ←
and
Calendars

WAKE UP, WALTER!

Walter needs to wake up at 6:10 in the morning.

Which alarm clock should he use?
Circle it.

DON'T BE LATE!

Ned delivers the newspaper.

He has to leave at 4:00 each morning.

Which clock shows the time he has to leave? Circle the correct clock.

WAKE UP, WALTER II

Walter's phone rang at 10:30 last night and woke him from a sound sleep. Which clock shows the time Walter woke up? Circle it.

Walter did not get back to sleep until 11:30. Draw a box ☐ around the clock that shows that time.

MAIL TIME!

On Monday, George mailed a letter to his pal Gracie. The letter took three days to reach her. On what day did Gracie get George's letter? Circle the day.

Monday

Tuesday

Wednesday

Thursday

Friday

Saturday

Sunday

OUT OF ORDER!

Can you put these days in order starting with Sunday? Write a **1**, **2**, **3**, **4**, **5**, **6** or **7** next to each day to put them in order.

Tuesday

Sunday

Friday

Monday

Saturday

Wednesday

Thursday

MISSING MONTH

Which month is missing. Circle it below.

January

February

March

?

May

June

December　　　　**July**
April　　　　**August**

MAIL TIME! II

Gracie got George's letter on Thursday and waited 12 days, starting Thursday, to write back. On which day did she write back? Circle the day.

Monday

Tuesday

Wednesday

Thursday

Friday

Saturday

Sunday

HAPPY BIRTHDAY

Can you put these famous birthdays in order? Write **1**, **2**, **3**, **4**, or **5** next to each date to put them in order.

Dr. Seuss: March 2

Oprah Winfrey: January 29

J. K. Rowling: July 31

Abraham Lincoln: February 12

William Shakespeare: April 23

HOLLY'S HOLIDAYS!

Can you help Holly put her holidays in order? Which holiday comes first in the year? Second? Third? Write **1**, **2**, or **3** next to each.

NEW YEAR'S DAY

FOURTH OF JULY

VALENTINE'S DAY

JULY	JANUARY	FEBRUARY
4	1	14

→Science←

ZIPPY ZEKE

Zeke wants to put these things in order from slowest to fastest.

Can you help him?

Write **1**, **2**, **3**, or **4** next to each picture to put them in order. Start with **1** for the slowest.

PLANET PUZZLER

Pete loves planets. Use the clues to help Pete label his picture of the planets.

- Mercury is next to the Sun.
- Mars is the farthest of these four planets from the Sun.
- Earth is next to Mars.
- Venus is next to Mercury.

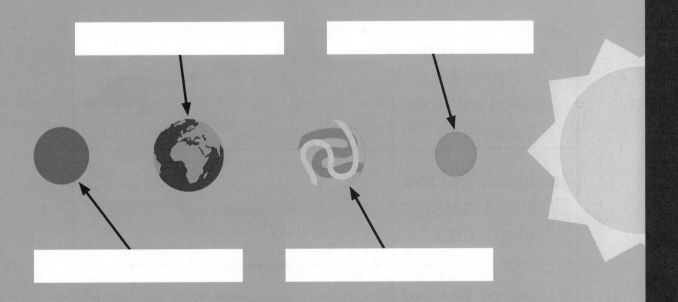

Venus   Mercury   Mars   Earth

TIME TWISTER

All dinosaurs did not live at the same time. Use the chart to answer these questions.

Could Compsognathus attack Plateosaurus?
☐ yes ☐ no

Could Ankylosaurus whack Tyrannosaurus with its tail? ☐ yes ☐ no

Could Tyrannosaurus chase Apatosaurus?
☐ yes ☐ no

Cretaceous Period 145–65 million years ago	Tyrannosaurus Ankylosaurus
Jurassic Period 205–144 million years ago	Apatosaurus Compsognathus
Triassic Period 248–206 million years ago	Coelophysis Plateosaurus

DOCTOR, DOCTOR!

Can you draw a line to match each word to the correct body part?

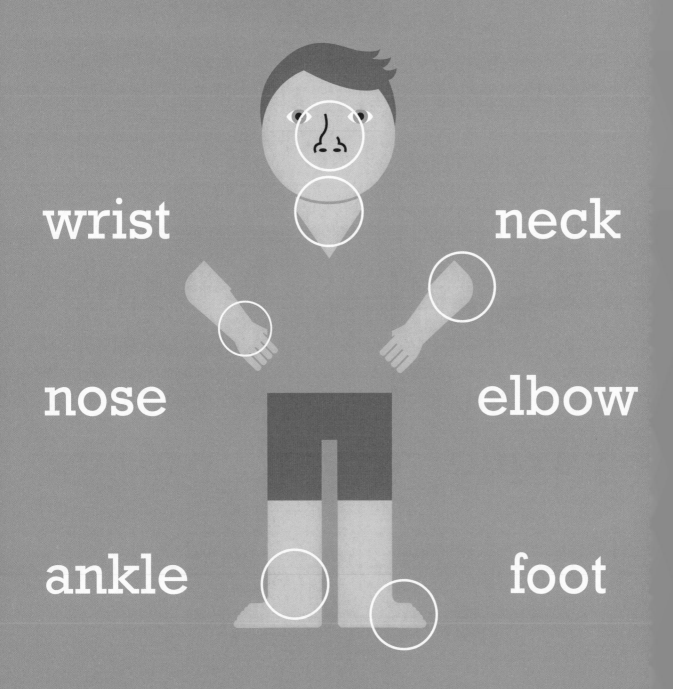

wrist

neck

nose

elbow

ankle

foot

COLOR MIX

What new color can you make with each combination? Write the correct color in each blank.

Yellow + **Blue** = _____

Yellow + **Red** = _____

Red + **Blue** = _____

purple   **green**   **orange**

BODY BASICS

Can you match each word to the correct body part? Draw lines to match the words to the body parts.

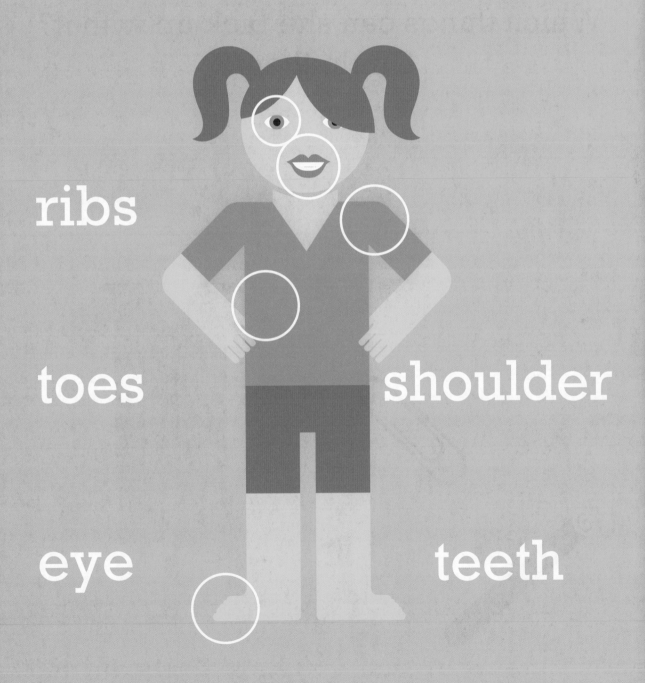

ribs

toes

shoulder

eye

teeth

STUCK ON YOU!

Molly has a magnet.
Which things can she pick up with it?
Circle them.

WATER, WATER EVERYWHERE!

Water can be a solid, a liquid, or a gas.

Which form do you see in each picture? Write the form in the blank.

solid   **liquid**   **gas**

NEEDY NED

Like all living things, Ned needs certain things to live.

Which of these things does he need? Circle them.

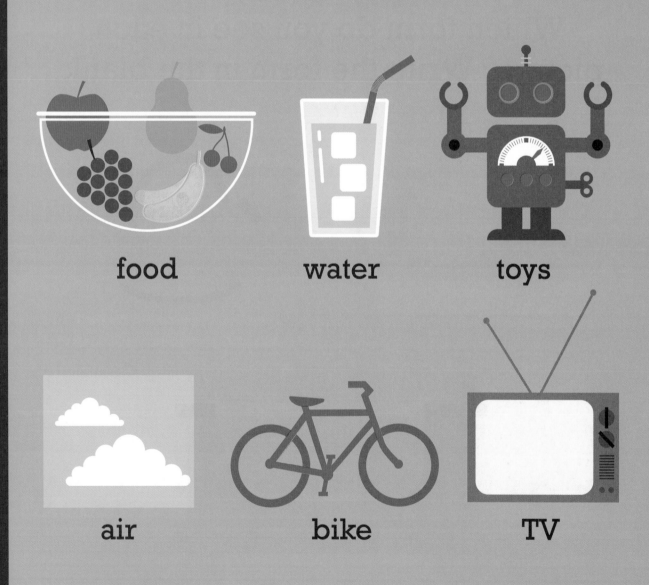

food water toys

air bike TV

PUSH OR PULL?

Penny and Paul are at the park. Which play things need a push to move? Write **push** below them.

Which need a pull? Write **pull** below them.

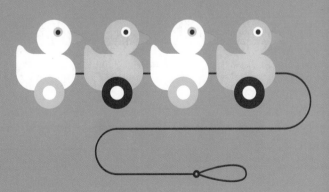

TRAIN RACE

The triplets are having a train race.
They each must push their trains
with the same force.

Circle the train that will win.

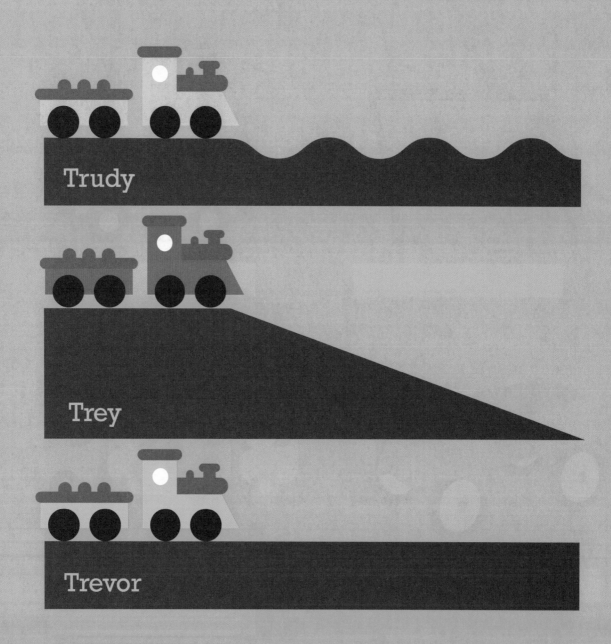

Trudy

Trey

Trevor

SPACE CASE

Austin the astronaut took pictures on his trip to space.

Write a label on each picture.

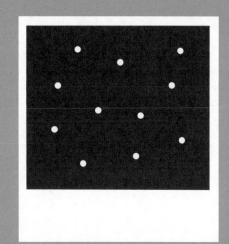

Earth   moon   stars   Mars

GOOD VIBES

Sound is made when things vibrate. Which instruments make sounds with vibrating strings? Circle them.

PUSH, PULL, OR TWIST?

Which of these actions requires a push?

Which one requires a pull?

Which one requires a twist?

Write **push**, **pull**, or **twist** below each.

SOLID SCIENCE

Which of the following pictures show only solids? Write an **S** below them.

GET ORGAN-IZED

Which two of these body organs do you need to digest your food? Draw a circle ◯ around the names.

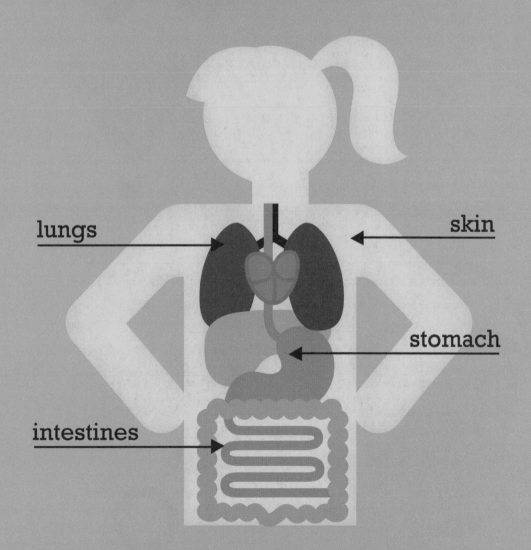

lungs

skin

stomach

intestines

Which organ helps you breathe? Draw a box ☐ around its name.

IT'S A GAS!

Which of the following objects contain a gas? Write a **G** below them.

Plants and Animals

BACKBONE OR NOT?

A vertebrate is an animal with a backbone.

Which of these animals are vertebrates? Circle them.

tuna

jellyfish

penguin

clam

seal

octopus

STAYING SAFE

Draw lines to match the animals with the way they stay safe.

porcupine fish

hard
shell

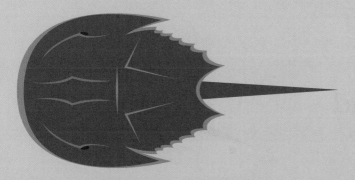

horseshoe crab

safety in
numbers

sharp
spines

school of fish

NO BACKBONE!

An invertebrate is an animal without a backbone.

Which of these sea animals are invertebrates? Circle them.

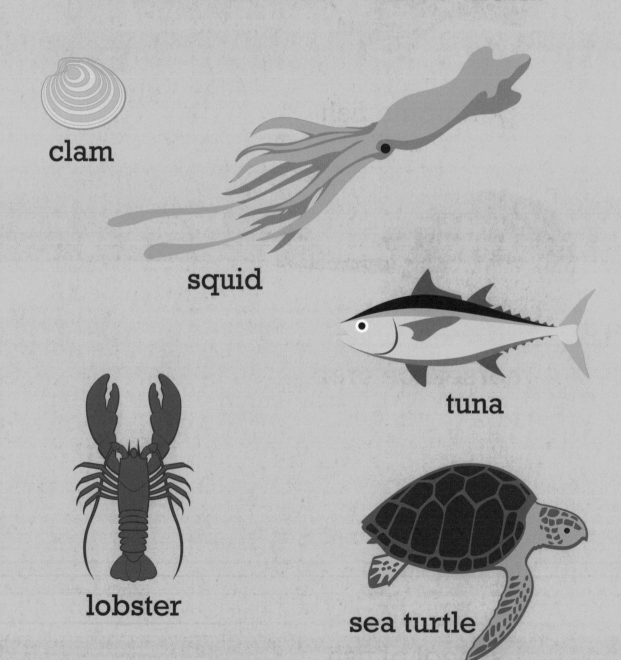

clam

squid

tuna

lobster

sea turtle

INSIDE A FISH

Label the parts of this fish.

Write the name of one part in each blank.

Then circle the name of the part that helps the fish breathe.

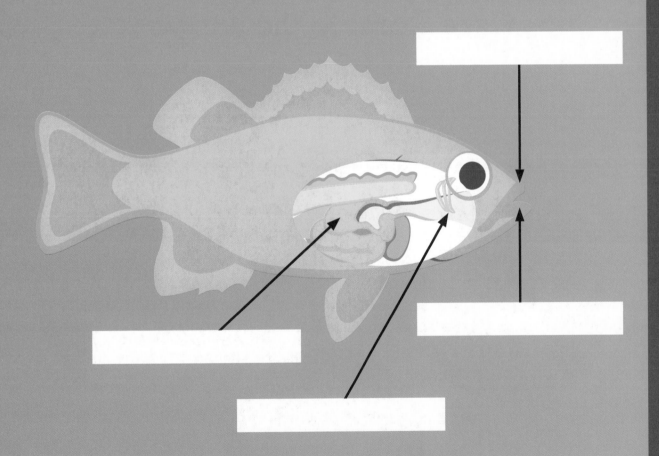

stomach   gills   mouth   nose

COOL COLONIES

Cora Coral has a soft body and a hard outer skeleton. Cora and other corals live together in colonies. What do these colonies form? Draw a line from Cora Coral to the answer.

volcano

cave

reef

TEENY TINY

Tiny animal and plant-like organisms are at the bottom of the ocean food chain.

Can you draw a line to match each tiny living thing to its name?

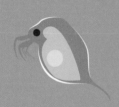

krill
(a tiny shrimp)

water flea

diatom
(a tiny plant)

WHAT AM I?

I have no brain or bones.

I have no heart or eyes.

My body is made up of
95 percent water.

I am a predator, a good hunter.

What am I? Circle me.

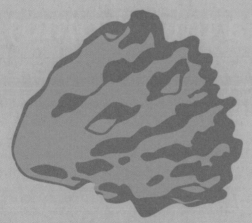

sponge

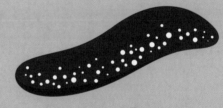

sea cucumber

scallop

jellyfish

ALL IN THE MANGROVE

Mangrove forests can be found along coastlines. Many animals call the mangrove home. Draw a line to match each animal to its name.

gray snapper

snake

tree crab

horseshoe crab

snowy egret

baby tarpon fish

spiny lobster

angel wing clam

DORA'S DOLPHIN

Dora drew a picture of a dolphin. Can you help her label its parts? Write the name of a part in each blank.

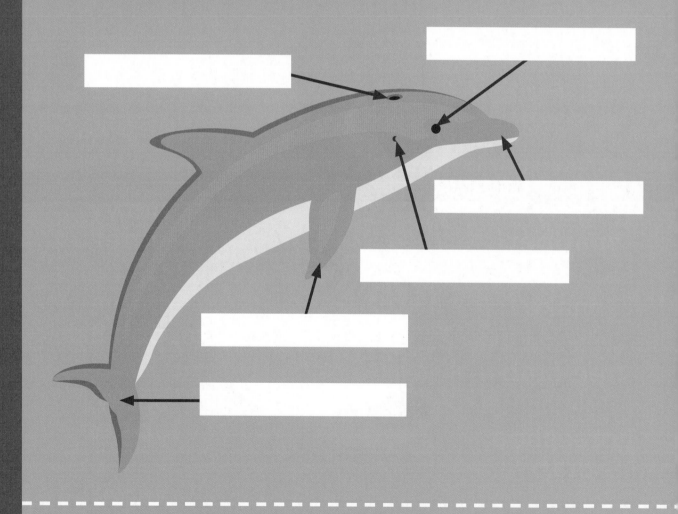

beak **eye** **ear**

flipper **blowhole** **flukes**

HEAVY WEIGHTS

Compare these marine animals. Can you draw a line to match each one to its correct weight?

great white shark

3½ tons

blue whale

15 tons

150 tons

whale shark

WHAT'S FOR DINNER?

A coral reef is made up of many thousands of tiny animals. Each one has a mouth surrounded by stingers.

Coral animals cannot move.

Which of these could be a coral animal's dinner? Circle them.

fish

shrimp

seaweed

clam

KNOW YOUR KELP

Kelp are very tall algae. They can stand upright in the water because they have small gas-filled balls, called gas bladders, on their stems.

Can you label the parts of this kelp? Draw a line to match each name to a part.

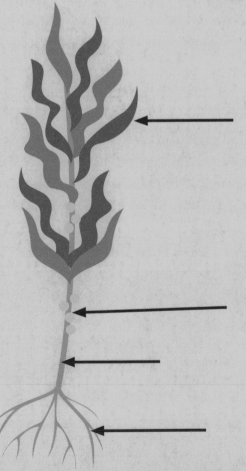

root (holdfast)

stem (stipe)

leaves (fronds)

gas bladder

A WHALE OF A TAIL

Lee went on a whale-watching trip. Help Lee write captions for his photos. Draw a line to match each photo to what the whale is doing.

**breaching
(jumping)**

tail slapping

**spyhopping
(looking around)**

**logging
(resting on water)**

OCEAN HABITATS

Millie collects pictures of ocean habitats. Draw a line from each picture to the name of the habitat.

seafloor

kelp forest

coral reef

polar sea

FIND THE PLANTS

Nate went on a nature walk and found some seeds. Which plants did they come from? Draw a line to match each seed to a plant.

BARNYARD BUMBLE

Farmer Sal likes to say the names of her animals. Only the animals are all mixed up! Can you draw a line to match each animal to its name?

horse

duck

pig

sheep

goat

OUT OF AFRICA

Annie just got back from a trip to Africa. Fill in the blanks to spell the names of four animals she saw there.

☐ lephan ☐

☐ ebr ☐

☐ iraff ☐

☐ io ☐

PLANT IT

Match each plant word to the correct picture.

seeds

grass

tree

leaf

flower

IT'S A STAGE

Here are some pictures of the life of a butterfly.

Write **1**, **2**, **3**, or **4** next to each picture to put them in order. Start with 1 for the smallest.

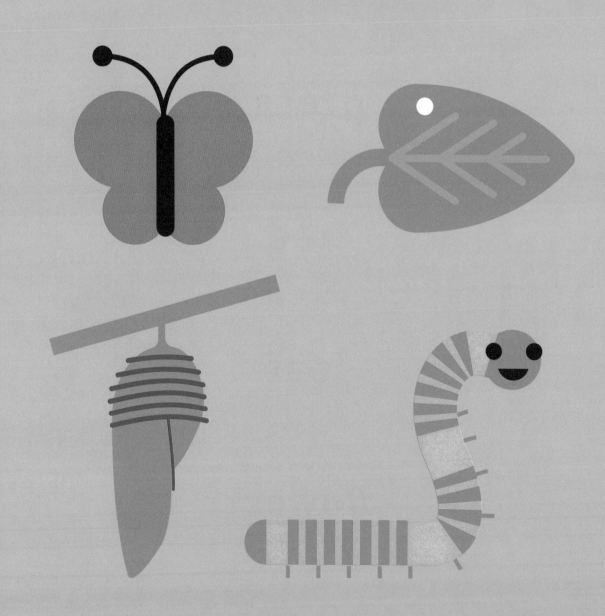

MISSING MAMAS

It's bedtime on the farm, but the babies can't find their mothers.

Can you match each mother to the correct baby name?

kid

foal

piglet

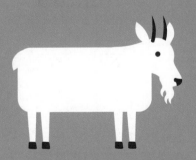

calf

HOME, SWEET HOME

Can you draw a line to match each animal to the place where it lives?

whale

toucan

rain forest

ocean

desert

tundra

polar bear

camel

BUG OFF!

Betsy goes buggy for bugs.
Can you help her match the correct name to each bug? Draw a line to make each match.

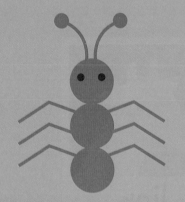  

beetle **fly** **ant** **dragonfly** **bee**

ALL MIXED UP

Sam saw lots of animals on his trip around the world, but he labeled his pictures wrong! Cross out Sam's labels and write the real animal name in the blank below each picture.

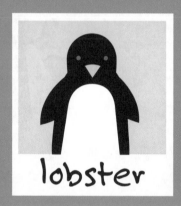

lobster

lion

giraffe

penguin

Circle the two animals Sam saw in Africa.

WAY TO GROW!

Pam and Pat are having a
plant-growing contest.

Circle the one who will win.

How do you know?

WHICH CAME FIRST?

Draw lines to connect the mothers and the babies. Write a **B** next to the baby in each pair.

FOOD CHAIN

Fred is drawing a food chain.
Can you help him put it in order?
Draw a line to put each animal in its
spot on the food chain.

EGG-CELLENT!

It's an animal egg hunt!
Can you figure out which eggs
belong to each animal? Draw a line to
connect each animal to its eggs.

LIZARD LEAP!

Lizzie Lizard wants to go to the Lizard Lounge. She can only leap to pictures of reptiles.

Draw a line to show her path.

Lizard Lounge

Lizzie can move across, down, and diagonally.

POND PALS

Mi Won has a pond in her yard.
Which of these plants and animals
might you see there? Circle them.

HOME, SWEET HOME II

Can you draw a line to match each animal to the place where it lives?

goat

penguin

African grassland

steep mountains

cold tundra

forest

deer

giraffe

FEATHERS OR FUR?

Zed the zookeeper has mixed up his mammals and birds.

Can you sort them out for him?

Write an **M** next to the mammals.
Write a **B** next to the birds.

FROG FUN

Write **1**, **2**, **3**, **4**, **5**, or **6** next to each picture to put them in order. Start with 1 for the youngest.

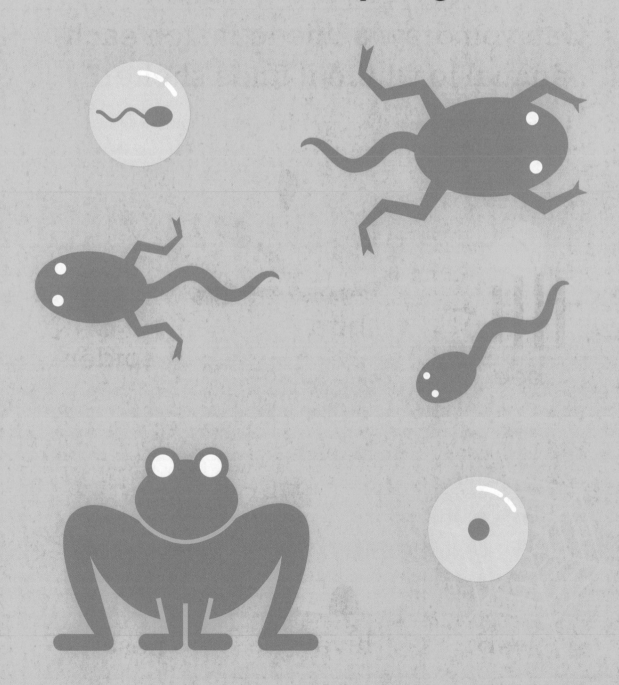

GIVE ME SHELTER

These animals want to go home.
Can you draw a line to match each
animal to where it finds shelter?

bee

bird

spider

web

hive

nest

GIVE ME SHELTER II

Which two of these animals find shelter in a tree?

Which ones find shelter in a burrow? Draw lines to match the animals to their habitats.

rabbit owl skunk squirrel

SEEDY STORY

Can you draw a line to match each seed to its parent plant?

ICE IS NICE

Which two of these animals would camouflage (blend in) best on snow or ice? Draw a circle ◯ around them.

leopard

polar bear

arctic fox

bat

Which one would camouflage best at night? Draw a box ☐ around it.

WILD THINGS!

Write a **W** next to the wild animals.
Write an **F** next to the ones you'd find
on a farm.

Earth and Weather

RAIN OR SNOW?

Storm clouds are coming! Charlie's thermometer says the temperature is 14°F. Will it rain or snow? Circle one.

rain   **snow**

32°

14°

Hint: Water freezes when the temperature drops below 32°F.

SKATE STORY

Skylar and Scotty want to ice-skate.
But they have to wait for their ponds
to freeze.

Circle the person who will
wait longer.

Skylar

Scotty

ICEBERG QUIZ

Icebergs float in the ocean. Is there more iceberg above the water surface or below? Check the box you think is right.

☐ Most is **under** the surface.

☐ Most is **above** the surface.

LAND OR SEA?

Joel says there is more land than ocean on Earth. Lanie says there is more ocean than land. Who is right? Check the box you think is right.

☐ More water

☐ More land

HOW'S THE WEATHER?

Draw a line to match each weather word to the correct picture.

rain

snow

wind

sunshine

cloud

WHAT DO I WEAR?

Hazel is the most fashionable kid on the block. She doesn't always dress for the right season, however. Which clothes should Hazel wear in the summer? Write an **S** below them.

WHAT DO I WEAR? II

Hazel is the most fashionable kid on the block. She doesn't always dress for the right season, however! Which items from her closet should she wear in the winter? Write a **W** by them.

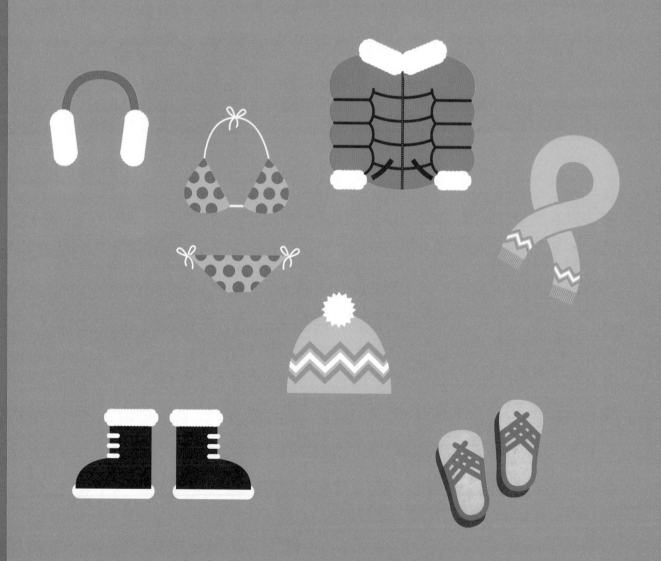

'TIS THE SEASON

Joe likes taking pictures of his backyard. He takes a picture whenever the seasons change.

Write the name of each season below the picture.

fall   winter   spring   summer

TOOL TIME

Tina uses different tools to learn about the weather.

Can you draw a line to match each tool to what it tells Tina?

temperature

wind direction

rainfall

EARTH DAY

Ernest is making an Earth Day poster.

Which pictures show ways to help the environment? Circle them.

WATER WORKS

Inga is doing a project on the water cycle. Can you help her write the labels on her poster? Two have been done for you already.

cloud

cloud

sun   water vapor   rain   lake

WEATHER WHOOPS!

Walter the weatherman is having trouble giving his report.

The weather symbols are mixed up on the TV screen.

Draw a line to match each type of weather to its picture.

blizzard

tornado

heat wave

thunderstorm

COLOR YOUR WORLD

Color all seven continents on this world map.

Color North America **blue**.
Color South America **orange**.

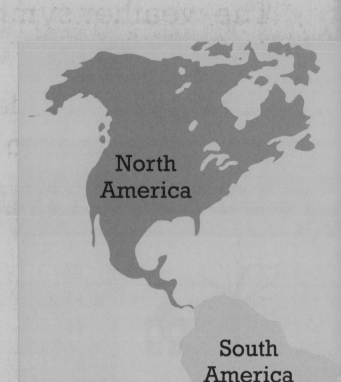

North America

South America

Color Africa **yellow**.
Color Europe **red**.
Color Asia **purple**.
Color Australia **green**.
Leave Antartica **white**.

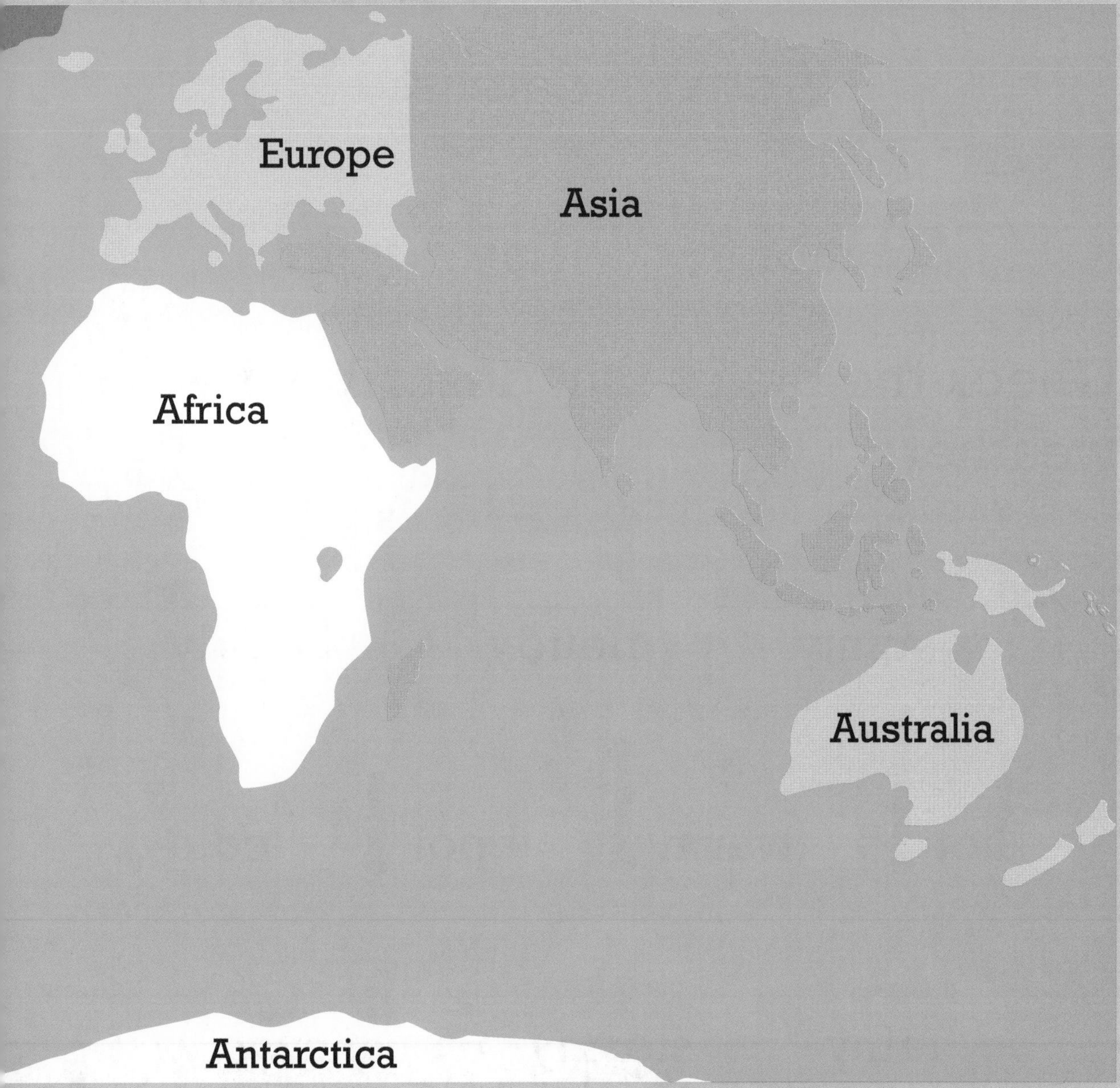

Europe

Asia

Africa

Australia

Antarctica

WEATHER REPORT

What's the weather like where you live right now? Be a weather reporter and fill out the chart below!

Today's date is:

month	day	year

Check the boxes that describe the weather:

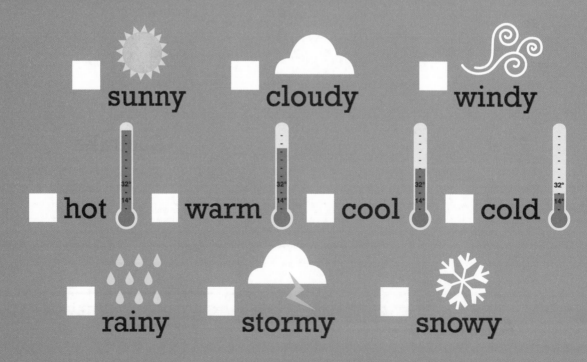

☐ sunny   ☐ cloudy   ☐ windy

☐ hot   ☐ warm   ☐ cool   ☐ cold

☐ rainy   ☐ stormy   ☐ snowy

Tomorrow's date is:

month	day	year

Tomorrow I predict it will be:

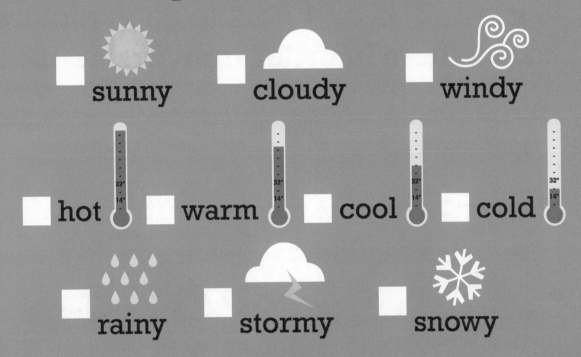

☐ sunny   ☐ cloudy   ☐ windy

☐ hot   ☐ warm   ☐ cool   ☐ cold

☐ rainy   ☐ stormy   ☐ snowy

Draw a picture of tomorrow's weather:

HOT LAVA

Laura loves volcanoes.

She took pictures of this volcano when it erupted.

Write **1**, **2**, **3**, or **4** next to each picture to put them in order from first to last.

→→ Dinosaurs ←←

NAME GAME

Deinonychus was a dinosaur.

Its name means "terrible claw."

Which picture shows Deinonychus?
Circle it.

SKELETON SEARCH

A vertebrate is an animal with a backbone. Think about what animals with backbones look like **today**.

Which of these ancient animals were vertebrates? Circle them.

Zalambdalestes

prehistoric jellyfish

Xiphactinus

Protoceratops

TREE TOPPER

These dinosaurs dined on different kinds of food.

Look at their body parts.

Which one could eat the leaves of tall trees? Circle it.

Triceratops

Brachiosaurus

Dilong

TRY THIS

Trilobites were ancient shelled animals.

Trilobite means "divided into three parts."

Can you find the trilobite? Write a **T** under it.

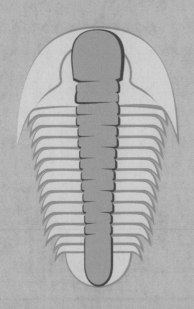

SO SPINELESS!

An invertebrate is an animal with no backbone.

Think about what animals **with** backbones look like. Which of these ancient animals did **not** have one? Circle them.

Buettneria

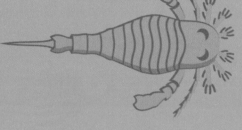

Eurypterid

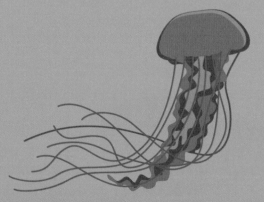

prehistoric jellyfish

prehistoric octopus

HIP CHECK

Dinosaurs stood up straight, with legs directly beneath them.

Most other reptiles have legs that stick out to the sides.

Can you find the two dinosaurs by looking at the way they stand? Write a **D** under them.

reptile stance

dinosaur stance

EGGS-ACTLY!

All these animals lived in dinosaur times.

Can you draw a line to match each animal to its eggs?

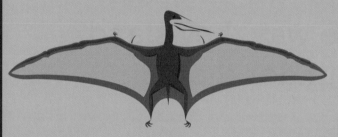

Pterosaur

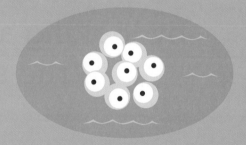

Protoceratops

prehistoric frog

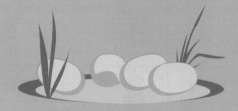

DINO-SORE!

These dinosaurs are named Stegoceras because of their oddly-shaped heads.

What do you think their name means? Circle the meaning.

flat top

horned roof

soft head

MEAT OR PLANTS

Meat-eaters have sharp teeth for tearing meat. Plant-eaters have mostly flat teeth for grinding plants.

Look at these dinosaur skulls.

Write an **M** below the meat-eaters. Write a **P** below the plant-eaters.

Kritosaurus

Dilophosaurus

Velociraptor

DINO DETECTIVE

Bobby is looking for body fossils.

Body fossils are parts of a living thing's body that have been preserved over time.

Can you help Bobby find the body fossils? Circle them.

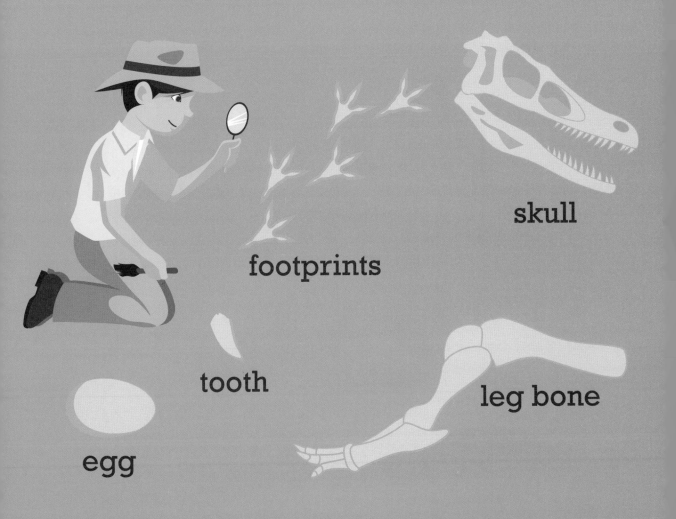

skull

footprints

tooth

leg bone

egg

DINO DETECTIVE II

Tracey is looking for trace fossils.

Trace fossils are not part of an animal.

They are fossils that show what a living thing was doing.

Can you help Tracey find the trace fossils? Circle them.

eggs

tooth

poop

footprint

MINI MAMMALS

Most of the mammals that lived at the same time as dinosaurs were no bigger than a small dog.

Which mammals lived with the dinosaurs? Circle them.

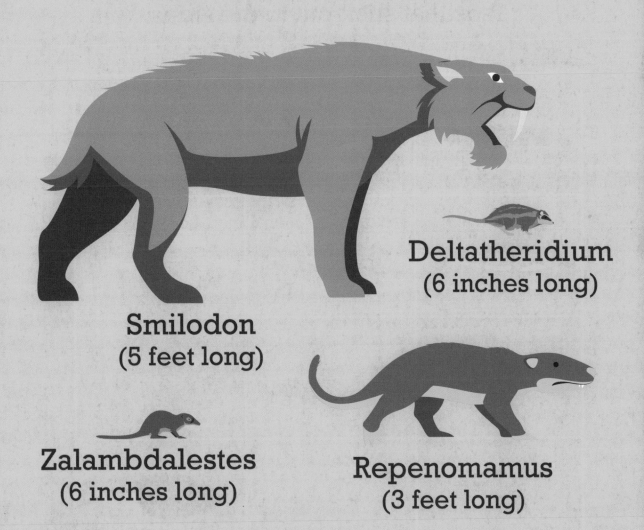

Deltatheridium
(6 inches long)

Smilodon
(5 feet long)

Zalambdalestes
(6 inches long)

Repenomamus
(3 feet long)

All lengths are approximate.

REPTILE REST

Reggie Reptile wants to cool off in the shade. He can only move to pictures of reptiles. Draw a line to show his path.

Hint: Most reptiles, other than dinosaurs, have legs that stick out to the sides.

Reggie can move across, down, and diagonally.

WHO AM I?

My name is Triceratops.

It means "a face with three horns."

Which dinosaur am I?

Write a **T** next to me.

EATING ON THE FLY

Pteranodon was a flying reptile that ate fish and possibly other animals.

Pteranodon swallowed fish whole.

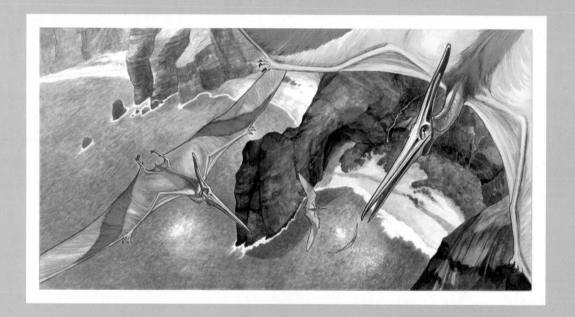

What bird today eats like this?
Circle it.

robin   pelican   duck

WHAT'S MAI NAME?

This is Maiasaura.

The picture gives a clue about how it got its name.

What do you think this dinosaur's name means? Circle the meaning.

big-toothed lizard

curious lizard

good-mother lizard

DINO DINER

Anton is drawing a food chain.
Can you help him put it in order?
Draw a line to put each animal
in its spot.

Segisaurus

Allosaurus

prehistoric
grasshopper

HOT STUFF

Some animals had plates or sails on their backs.

These may have absorbed heat from the sun.

Which animals may have warmed up this way? Circle them.

Sinornithosaurus

Spinosaurus

Stegosaurus

DINO DEFENSE

This is Ankylosaurus.

Can you circle three body parts that it used to protect itself?

Look at the list below for ideas.

club on tail

horns on head

spikes on ankles

big teeth

spikes on back

long, sharp claws

NAB THE NIPPER

Some dinosaurs had beaklike mouths. They nipped the leaves off small bushes.

Look at the dinosaur skulls.

Which dinosaur was the nipper? Write an **N** below the nipper. Write an **M** below the dinosaur who ate meat.

Ankylosaurus

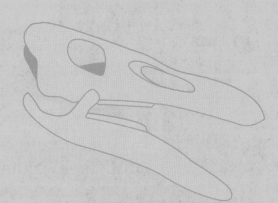

Anatotitan

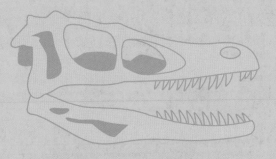

Velociraptor

TRACE RACE

Pete the paleontologist is looking for a fossil skeleton. He can only move to pictures of **trace fossils**.

Can you draw a line to help him find his way?

Hint: Trace fossils show what a living thing was doing. They are not pieces of the actual animal.

prints	tooth	bone	skull
claw	poop	nest	bone
prints	skull	claw	print
skull	egg	tooth	poop

Pete can move across, down, and diagonally.

ROCK ON!

Rocky is looking for fossils in sedimentary rock.

The layers of sedimentary rock build up over time.

Where can he find the oldest fossils? Draw a circle ◯ around them. Draw a box ☐ around the youngest fossils.

READY, SET, JET

While dinosaurs roamed the earth, other animals lived in the sea.

Some moved by taking in water and squirting it out. This made them **jet** through the water.

Can you find the jetters below? Circle them.

ammonite

prehistoric frog

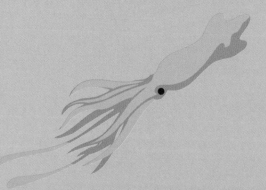

prehistoric squid

prehistoric octopus

CREATURE FEATURE

These prehistoric creatures have something to say for themselves.

Can you draw a line to match each creature to its quote?

Pteranodon

1. Scientists do not consider me a dino.

Velociraptor

2. My name means "arm lizard" because my arms are longer than my legs.

3. I am famous for my hunting skills.

Brachiosaurus

MAZIE'S MAZE

Mazie wants to steal a dinosaur egg to feed her babies. She can only move to pictures of mammals.

Can you draw a line to show Mazie the right path?

Hint: Mammals have fur.

Mazie can move across, down, and diagonally.

BABY ON BOARD

Brachiosaurus traveled in herds.

The young stayed in the middle of the herd for protection.

Which of the tracks show how these dinosaurs traveled? Circle them.

Write a **Y** below the tracks of the young dinosaurs.

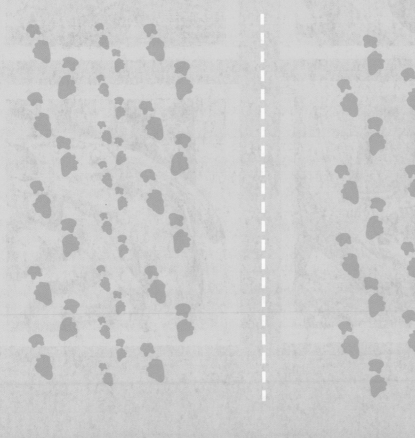

WE ARE FAMILY

Gigantoraptor belongs to a family of birdlike dinosaurs.

Which dinosaur is the Gigantoraptor?

Circle it.

MINI MAMMALS

Mammals from dinosaur times were very small.

Which mammal did not live during the time of dinosaurs? Draw an **X** through it.

Circle the smallest mammal.

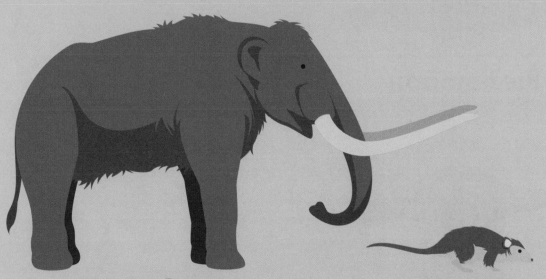

Mastodon
(15 feet long)

Eomaia
(5 inches long)

Megazostrodon
(4 inches long)

Gobiconodon
(18 inches long)

Animals not drawn to scale.

HOME, SWEET HOME

These ancient animals are lost!

Can you draw a line to help each one find its home?

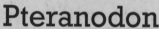

Pteranodon

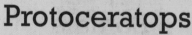

Protoceratops

Plesiosaurus

➡ Transportation ⬅

LAND, SEA, OR SKY?

Some of these vehicles go on land. Some go in the sky, and some go in the sea.

Draw lines to the words to show which vehicles go where.

sky

land

sea

WAY TO GO!

Write **1**, **2**, **3**, **4**, or **5** next to each picture to put them in order from fastest to slowest. Start with 1 for the **fastest**.

NAME THAT BOAT

Draw a line to match each boat with its name.

sailboat

canoe

motor boat

row boat

IT'S A SIGN

The train is coming!
Which sign tells the driver to stop at the tracks? Draw a circle ◯ around it.

Which sign tells the driver that deer may cross the road? Draw a box ☐ around it.

LIGHT THE WAY

Rita Racer is trying to get home fast.
Look at the traffic signals.
Which path is the **fastest**? Circle it.

PIECE ME TOGETHER

Lou and his crew are building something that goes.

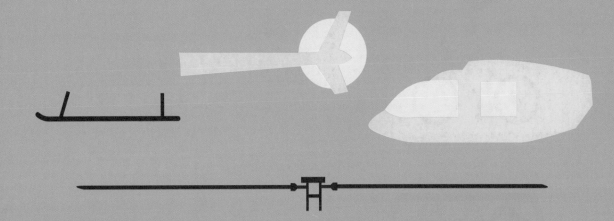

Use the parts to draw a complete vehicle here.

Circle the name:

ship   helicopter   plane   rocket

SAFETY FIRST

Connect each picture to the way to make the person safer.

Two pictures have the same answer.

Wear a helmet

Sit down

Wear a seatbelt

→ Games ←
and Puzzles

SCRAMBLE-O-SAURUS

Unscramble the letters to solve each clue below. Then use the numbered letters to answer the riddle.

1. The preserved remains or traces of a plant or animal

   ☐☐☐☐☐☐
     4 5

   silofs

2. An animal hunted by others

   ☐☐☐☐
   2 3

   yepr

3. An animal that hunts others

   ☐☐☐☐☐☐☐☐
      1 6

   toparred

4. An extinct animal that stood upright

   ☐☐☐☐☐☐☐☐
       7

   rindaosu

Which dinosaur always had an umbrella?

☐☐☐☐☐☐☐☐☐
1 2 3 4 5 6 7 2 7 5

VOLCANO!

Use the clues to figure out the name of each dinosaur. Then put the numbered letters in order to solve this riddle.

1. I had a large head and small arms.

☐☐☐☐☐☐☐☐☐☐☐☐☐
       4

2. I looked like a tank.

☐☐☐☐☐☐☐☐☐☐☐☐☐
    6 5

3. I was a small and fast hunter.

☐☐☐☐☐☐☐☐☐☐☐☐
3   1

4. I had a small head and a long neck.

☐☐☐☐☐☐☐☐☐☐☐☐☐
  2

What did the dino say when the volcano erupted?

What a ☐☐☐☐ - ☐☐ day!
    1 2 3 4 5 6

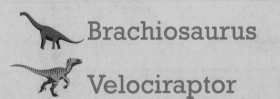 Brachiosaurus   Tyrannosaurus

Velociraptor   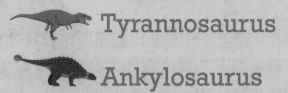 Ankylosaurus

GO FISH!

In this game, the person with the most pairs wins.

Who will win this round?
Circle the winner.

Jack's cards

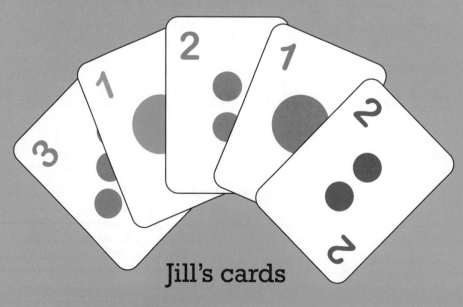

Jill's cards

Jack and Jill are playing another round, and this time, you're playing!

Jack's cards

Jill's cards

Circle the card you need to win.

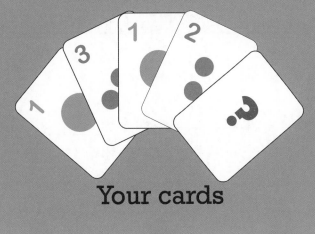

Your cards

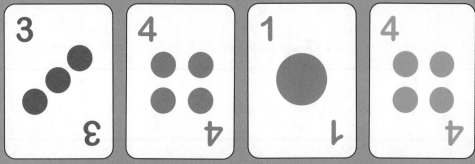

OCEAN PUZZLER

Unscramble the letters to solve each clue below. Then use the numbered letters to answer the riddle.

1. A movement of ocean water that reaches land.

vewa

```
  3 4
```

2. This ocean animal is a mammal.

poldinh

```
  8 2 5
```

3. These tiny animals have hard skeletons that can form a reef.

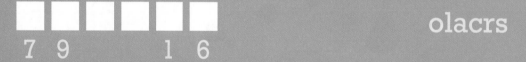

olacrs

```
7 9     1 6
```

Why are fish so smart?

Because they

!

```
1 2 3 4   2 5   6 7 8 9 9 1 6
```

TERMITE TRIP

Ted the termite wants to get to the house. He can only crawl on pictures of words that begin with **t**. Can draw a line to you help him find the path?

He can only go down or across.

WORD PUZZLES

Paula has some puzzle pieces. Can you make 9 words with her pieces? Write them below.

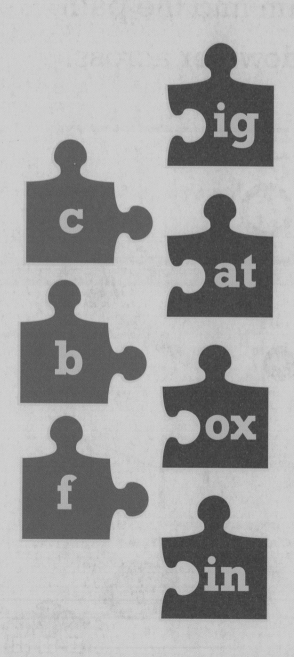

Can you make 12 more words with these pieces? Write them below.

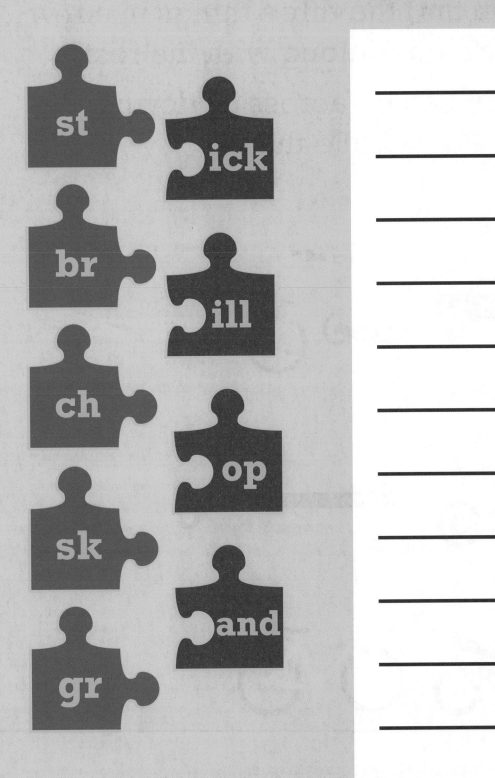

st · ick
br · ill
ch · op
sk · and
gr

MOVE IT

Can you find the three things in a row that do not belong with the rest?

You can go across or down.
Circle them.

TIC-TAC-GO

Can you find the three things in a row that do not belong with the rest?
You can go across or down.
Circle them.

BUGGY BUSINESS

Can you circle the two ladybugs that are exactly the same?

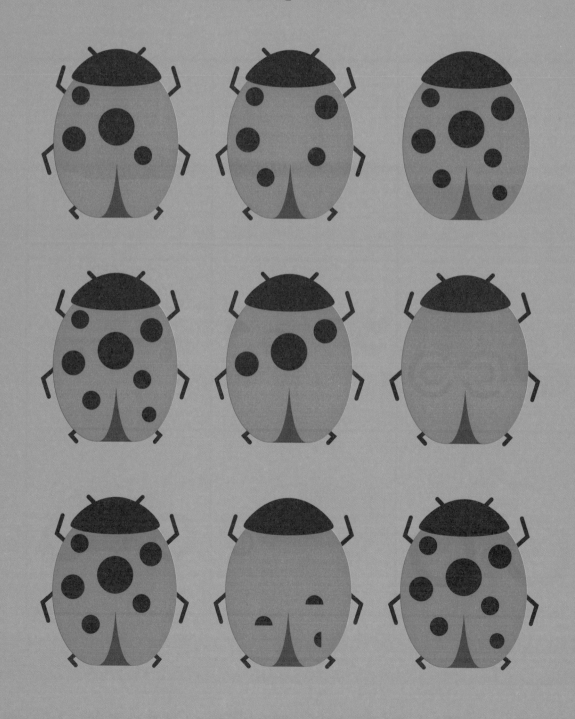

→→ Answers ←←

RHYMING RIDDLE

Can you circle the item that finishes this rhyming riddle?

Some are red.
Some are blue.
It's on your foot.
It's a _____.

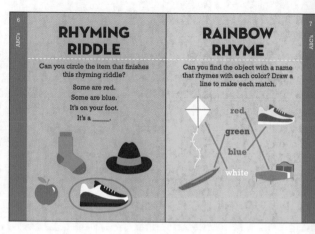

RAINBOW RHYME

Can you find the object with a name that rhymes with each color? Draw a line to make each match.

red
green
blue
white

RHYME TIME

Draw lines to match the animals that have rhyming names.

dog   rat
whale   frog
cat   snail

RHYME TIME II

Can you find a food that rhymes with each animal's name? Draw a line to make each match.

parrot   ape   snake
grape   cake   carrot

LINE UP

Coach Talia is picking players for the team.

Draw a line to match each player to the word that describes her.

2   3   7

tall   taller   tallest

CIRCUS CLAPS

Words can be divided into parts called **syllables**.

To find the syllables, clap as you speak the parts of each word.

tiger   clown
seal   acrobat

Circle the one who gets the most claps. Write the number here:
3 claps

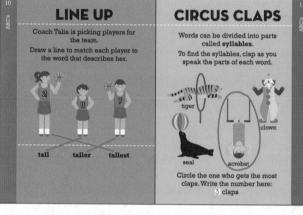

SARA'S SNACK

Sara only eats foods with two syllables.

Clap as you say each part of the words to count the syllables.

Circle the foods that Sara will eat.

spaghetti   apple   carrot
broccoli   pretzel
milk

TWO IN ONE

Can you find the two smaller words in each big word? Write them on the lines below each word.

cupcake
cup | cake

football
foot | ball

mailbox
mail | box

ladybug
lady | bug

RHYMING RIDDLE II

Can you circle the item that finishes this rhyming riddle?

It drives in mud.
It won't get stuck.
It's not a car.
It's a _____.

WHAT'S THE STORY?

Which words go best with the picture? Draw a line from the picture to the words that match.

1. Mac is a cat. He is in a hat.
2. Mac is a man. He has a hat.

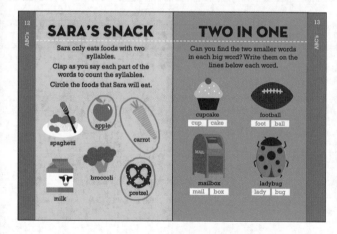

SYLLABLES WITH SYLVIA

Sylvia's name has three syllables.

That means you clap three times when you say the parts of her name.

How many names with three syllables can you find below? Circle them.

elephant   tiger   bear
crocodile   monkey   kangaroo

MISSING MUSIC

These instruments are missing the first letters of their names. The letters are all at the bottom of the page. Write the missing letters in the blanks.

g uitar
d rum
t rumpet
p iano
v iolin

v g t p d

LOST LETTERS

Write in the missing letters to complete the name of each animal. You can find the letters at the bottom of the page.

P enguin   S eal
sea t urtle   sea h orse
O tter   w hale

o h w p s t

CREATURE FEATURE

Each of these sea animals has something to say.

Can you draw a line to match each animal to its quote?

1. As I grow bigger, I have to find a new home.
2. My webbed toes make me a good swimmer.
3. I may look dangerous, but I am harmless.

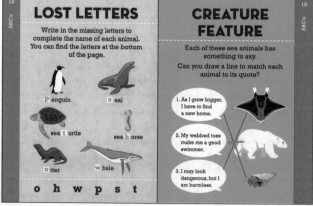
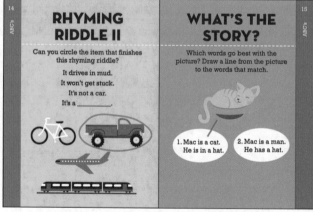

CHOPPED FRUIT

The names of these fruits have been chopped in two! Draw lines to match the parts.

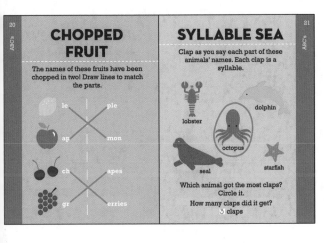

le — ple
ap — mon
ch — apes
gr — erries

SYLLABLE SEA

Clap as you say each part of these animals' names. Each clap is a syllable.

lobster
dolphin
octopus
seal
starfish

Which animal got the most claps? Circle it.

How many claps did it get?
3 claps

LET'S PLAY CARDS!

Sam and Pam are playing a game. The winner makes the most pairs that rhyme.

Draw lines to connect the rhyming pairs. Circle the winner.

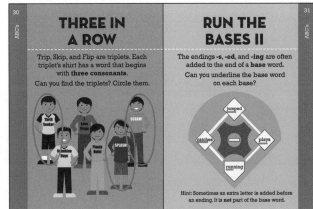

dog   moose   frog   duck   goose
Pam's Cards

bat   bee   bear   ant   rat
Sam's Cards

23

CLEAN UP

Claire is cleaning out her closet. She is organizing her things by the **first** letter of their names.

Draw lines to put each item in its box.

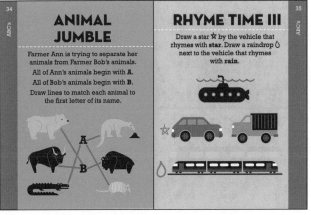

C   S   B

BLEND BUSTER

These words are missing their beginning blends.
Write the correct blend in each blank.

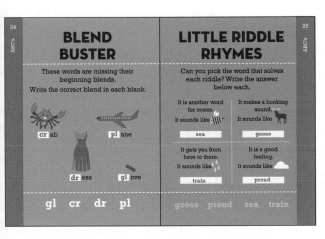

cr ab
pl ane
dr ess
gl ove

gl   cr   dr   pl

25

LITTLE RIDDLE RHYMES

Can you pick the word that solves each riddle? Write the answer below each.

It is another word for ocean.
It sounds like
sea

It makes a honking sound.
It sounds like
goose

It gets you from here to there.
It sounds like
train

It is a good feeling.
It sounds like
proud

goose   proud   sea   train

CONTRACTION ACTION

A **contraction** is a short way of writing two words as one.

Read the words on each wheel. Which contractions are made with the word in the center? Circle them.

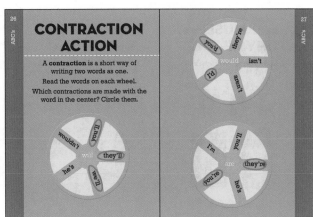

you'd   they're   would   isn't   I'd   aren't

wouldn't   I'll   you'll   he's   will   they'll   we'll

27

I'm   you'll   are   they're   you're   he's

CONTRACTION ACTION II

Read the words on each wheel. Which contractions are made with the word in the center? Circle them.

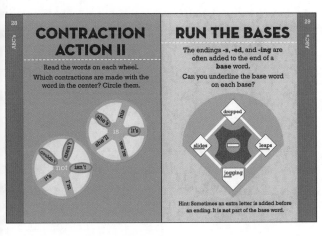

she's   I'm   is   it's   she'll   we're   aren't   couldn't   isn't   it's   not   I'm

RUN THE BASES

The endings **-s**, **-ed**, and **-ing** are often added to the end of a **base** word.

Can you underline the base word on each base?

dropped
slides   leaps
jogging

Hint: Sometimes an extra letter is added before an ending. It is **not** part of the base word.

THREE IN A ROW

Trip, Skip, and Flip are triplets. Each triplet's shirt has a word that begins with **three consonants**.

Can you find the triplets? Circle them.

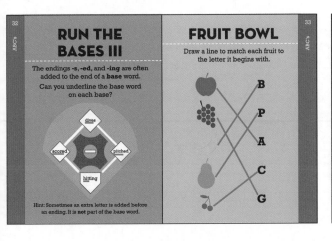

Thrill Seeker
Love Frogs
Sunshine Days
SCRAM!
Plants Rule!
SPLASH!

RUN THE BASES II

The endings **-s**, **-ed**, and **-ing** are often added to the end of a **base** word.

Can you underline the base word on each base?

jumped
catches   plays
running

Hint: Sometimes an extra letter is added before an ending. It is **not** part of the base word.

RUN THE BASES III

The endings **-s**, **-ed**, and **-ing** are often added to the end of a **base** word.

Can you underline the base word on each base?

dives
scored   pitched
hitting

Hint: Sometimes an extra letter is added before an ending. It is **not** part of the base word.

FRUIT BOWL

Draw a line to match each fruit to the letter it begins with.

B
P
A
C
G

ANIMAL JUMBLE

Farmer Ann is trying to separate her animals from Farmer Bob's animals.

All of Ann's animals begin with **A**.
All of Bob's animals begin with **B**.

Draw lines to match each animal to the first letter of its name.

A
B

RHYME TIME III

Draw a star ✰ by the vehicle that rhymes with **star**. Draw a raindrop ⬭ next to the vehicle that rhymes with **rain**.

SOUNDS LIKE...

Two of these objects have names that sound the same. Draw a line between the two objects whose names sound the same.

FLOUR

WHICH DOES NOT BELONG?

The words in each boat below are supposed to be alike in some way. Which word does not belong in each boat? Circle it.

TUNE TIME

WHICH THREE INSTRUMENTS HAVE STRINGS? WRITE THEIR NAMES BELOW.

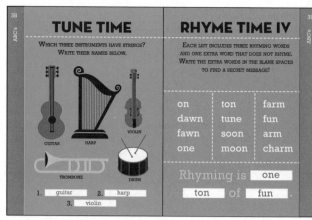

GUITAR HARP VIOLIN

TROMBONE DRUM

1. guitar 2. harp
3. violin

RHYME TIME IV

EACH LIST INCLUDES THREE RHYMING WORDS AND ONE EXTRA WORD THAT DOES NOT RHYME. WRITE THE EXTRA WORDS IN THE BLANK SPACES TO FIND A SECRET MESSAGE!

on	ton	farm
dawn	tune	fun
fawn	soon	arm
one	moon	charm

Rhyming is one
ton of fun

ART MUSEUM RHYME TIME

Which of the things shown rhyme with **blue**? Circle them.

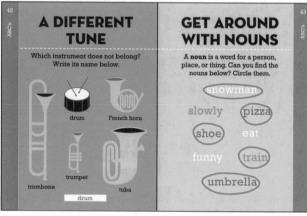

BARNYARD RHYME TIME

Can you find the animals with names that rhyme with **fog**? Write their names below.

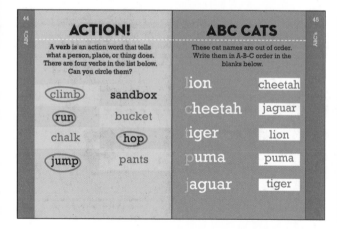

donkey dog
duck frog sheep

1. dog 2. frog

A DIFFERENT TUNE

Which instrument does not belong? Write its name below.

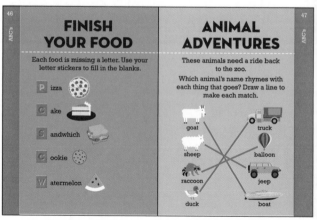

drum French horn
trumpet
trombone tuba

drum

GET AROUND WITH NOUNS

A **noun** is a word for a person, place, or thing. Can you find the nouns below? Circle them.

snowman
slowly pizza
shoe eat
funny train
umbrella

ACTION!

A **verb** is an action word that tells what a person, place, or thing does. There are four verbs in the list below. Can you circle them?

climb sandbox
run bucket
chalk hop
jump pants

ABC CATS

These cat names are out of order. Write them in A-B-C order in the blanks below.

lion cheetah
cheetah jaguar
tiger lion
puma puma
jaguar tiger

FINISH YOUR FOOD

Each food is missing a letter. Use your letter stickers to fill in the blanks.

P izza
C ake
S andwhich
C ookie
W atermelon

ANIMAL ADVENTURES

These animals need a ride back to the zoo.

Which animal's name rhymes with each thing that goes? Draw a line to make each match.

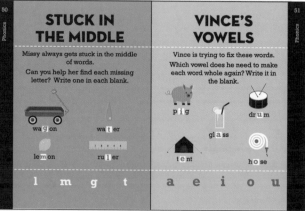

goat truck
sheep balloon
raccoon jeep
duck boat

TALK ABOUT TRAINS

Which word describes each train? Write the word in the blank below each train.

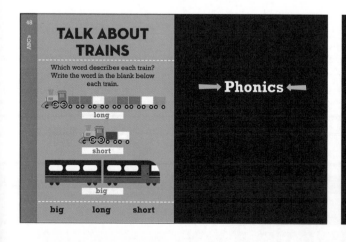

long
short
big

big long short

→ Phonics ←

STUCK IN THE MIDDLE

Missy always gets stuck in the middle of words.

Can you help her find each missing letter? Write one in each blank.

wa g on wa t er
lem o n ru l er

l m g t

VINCE'S VOWELS

Vince is trying to fix these words. Which vowel does he need to make each word whole again? Write it in the blank.

p i g dr u m
gl a ss
t e nt h o se

a e i o u

MIDDLE MATCH

Say the name of each animal. Then read the sentence below it.

Which word in the sentence has the same **middle** sound as the animal's name? Circle it.

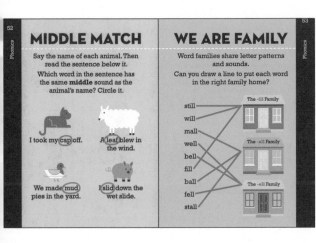

I took my **cap** off.

A leaf blew in the wind.

We made **mud** pies in the yard.

I **slid** down the wet slide.

WE ARE FAMILY

Word families share letter patterns and sounds.

Can you draw a line to put each word in the right family home?

still
will
mall
well
bell
fill
ball
fell
stall

The -ill Family

The -all Family

The -ell Family

MAY DAY

Jay made up a poem about his favorite month: May.

Can you find all the words that have the long **a** sound, as in **May**? Circle them.

May Day
You can enjoy May
in so many ways
You can sail on the lake
on warm, windy days

You can walk in the rain
and make up a game,
Or, stay in your house
and play games just the same!

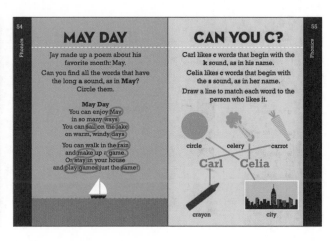

CAN YOU C?

Carl likes **c** words that begin with the **k** sound, as in his name.

Celia likes **c** words that begin with the **s** sound, as in her name.

Draw a line to match each word to the person who likes it.

circle   celery   carrot

Carl   **Celia**

crayon   city

WE ARE FAMILY II

Word families share letter patterns and sounds. Draw lines to put each word in the correct family home.

nest
boat
best
meat
coat
goat
seat
vest
beat

The -o mily

The -eat Family

The -est Family

I SPY!

Mike likes to play I Spy. He spies only words that have the long **i** sound, as in his name.

Write the answer to each of Mike's clues in the blank below it.

I spy something you ride.
bike

I spy something my dad wears to work.
tie

I spy a number.
nine

I spy a place where bees live.
hive

hive   train   bike   tie
nine   six   hill   suit

QUICK CHANGE

These words are changing letters! Then they become new words.

Which picture solves each problem? Draw a line to make each match. The first one has been done for you.

hat   Change **h** to **b** =
cap   Change **p** to **t** = ?
top   Change **t** to **m** = ?
clap   Change **a** to **i** = ?
ball   Change **a** to **e** = ?

STIR IT UP

Vern is making soup.

Which pots only have words that have the same **r-controlled** sound as Vern's name? Circle them.

storm clerk

whir hurt

bird turn her

sir deer fur

JUNE TUNE

June made up a song about her favorite month: June!

Can you find all the words that have the long **u** sound, as in **June**? Circle them.

June
It has clear blue skies,
fresh fruits and juice,
It has bright tie-ayes
and cute bathing suits

It has barbecues
and sandy dunes
It has happy tunes—
and it's called June!

DROP A LETTER

These words are dropping letters! Then they become new words.

Which picture solves each problem? Draw a line to make each match. The first one has been done for you.

scar – s = ?
chat – c = ?
pant – p = ?
snail – s = ?
train – t = ?

CLUSTER BUSTER

Sly is a sneak! He has swiped the **s clusters** from the beginnings of these words.

Write the correct blend in each blank.

spoon   **sl**ide

smile   **sc**arf

sp   sc   sl   sm

ZANY ZOO

Jack and Judd care for animals whose names have a **short** vowel sound, like their names.

Jake and Julie care for animals whose names have a **long** vowel sound, like their names.

Draw lines to put each animal with the correct zookeepers.

duck   ape   skunk

Jack + Judd   Jake + Julie

ox   mule

WATCH OUT!

The letters **ow** can make the sound **ow**, as in **cow**, or the long **o** sound, as in **slow**.

This cow wants to get back to the barn. Which path only has words that make the same sound as **cow**? Draw the path.

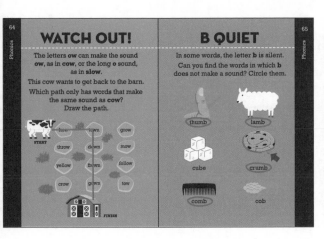

START   bow   town   grow
throw   down   mow
yellow   frown   follow
crow   gown   tow
FINISH

B QUIET

In some words, the letter **b** is silent.

Can you find the words in which **b** does not make a sound? Circle them.

thumb   lamb

cube   crumb

comb   cob

END BLENDS

The blends have fallen off the ends of these words!

Write the correct blend in each blank.

te**nt**   sta**mp**   ma**sk**

tru**nk**   si**ng**   li**st**

nk   mp   ng
nt   sk   st

O.K. CORRAL

These **k** words are on the loose. In some of the words, the letter **k** is silent.

Can you round up the words in which **k** does not make a sound? Draw a line from each silent-k word to the lasso.

king   kite
key   kitten   knob
knot
knit   knife
knight

68 · Phonics · ADD A LETTER

These words are adding letters in order to become new words!
Which picture solves each problem?
Draw a line to make each match.
The first one has been done for you.

g + love =
c + lock = ?
w + heel = ?
pl + ant = ?
sp + ring = ?

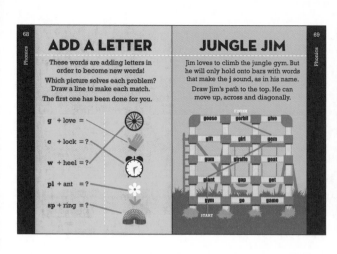

69 · JUNGLE JIM

Jim loves to climb the jungle gym. But he will only hold onto bars with words that make the **j** sound, as in his name.
Draw Jim's path to the top. He can move up, across and diagonally.

FINISH

goose	gerbil	give
gift	girl	gem
gum	giraffe	goat
giant	gap	get
gym	go	game

START

70 · Phonics · SHARK BAIT

Sharif is fishing for sharks.
The sharks in these parts only bite lures with **sh** on them.
Which lures will the Shark bite? Circle them.

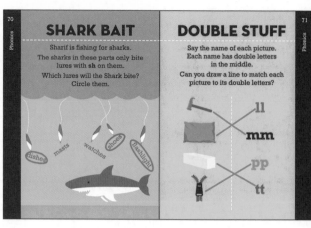

dishes · masts · watches · shoes · flashlight

71 · DOUBLE STUFF

Say the name of each picture.
Each name has double letters in the middle.
Can you draw a line to match each picture to its double letters?

ll
mm
pp
tt

72 · Phonics · SO SWEET

Swifty is good at lots of sports. But his best sport begins with the letters **sw**.
Which sport is Swifty's sweetest?
Write **SW** below it.

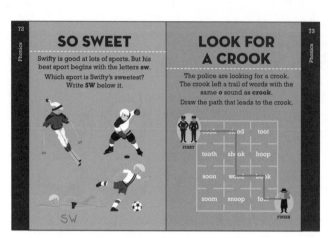

SW

73 · Phonics · LOOK FOR A CROOK

The police are looking for a crook.
The crook left a trail of words with the same **o** sound as **crook**.
Draw the path that leads to the crook.

START

cook	stood	toot
tooth	shook	hoop
soon	wood	book
zoom	snoop	foot

FINISH

74 · Phonics · READY OAR NOT

Corey and Tory are going to row across the pond. They need to choose the two oars that have only words with the **or** sound.
Which oars do they need?
Color them brown.

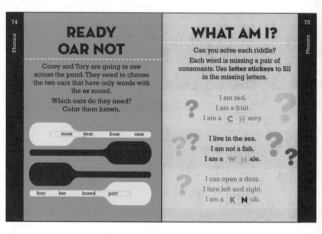

| more | your | boar | care |
| four | her | bored | port |

75 · Phonics · WHAT AM I?

Can you solve each riddle?
Each word is missing a pair of consonants. Use **letter stickers** to fill in the missing letters.

? I am red.
I am a fruit.
I am a **C H** erry. ?

?? I live in the sea.
I am not a fish.
I am a **W H** ale. ??

? I can open a door.
I turn left and right.
I am a **K N** ob.

76 · Phonics · IT'S E-Z

Can you find the picture that shows what each word will turn into when you add a final **e**? Draw a line to make each match.

kit
tap
cub
cap

77 · Phonics · D-DAY

The animals are loose! Farmer Dan from The Dandy Dude Ranch is trying to collect his animals. Put a **D** sticker on all the animals that begin with **D**.

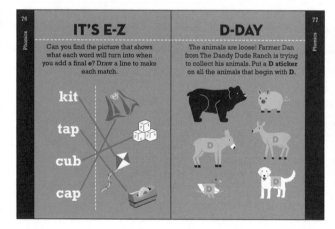

78 · Phonics · STUCK ON VOWELS

These vehicles are stuck without their vowels. Add **letter stickers** to fill in the missing vowels.

ball **O O** n
r **A** ce c **A** r
b **U** s
tra **I** n
plan **E**

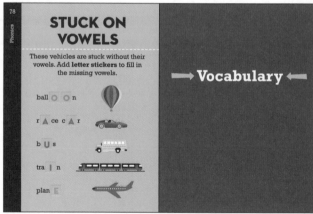

→ Vocabulary ←

80 · Vocabulary · WORD PARTY

A **noun** is a person, place, or thing.
A **verb** is a word that tells what a person or thing does. Write an **N** next to all the nouns in this word party.
Write a **V** next to the verbs.

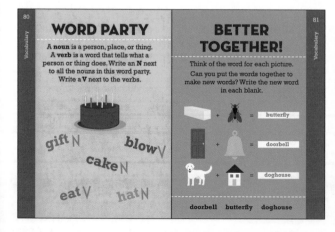

gift **N** · blow **V** · cake **N** · eat **V** · hat **N**

81 · BETTER TOGETHER!

Think of the word for each picture.
Can you put the words together to make new words? Write the new word in each blank.

+ = butterfly
+ = doorbell
+ = doghouse

doorbell · butterfly · doghouse

82 · Vocabulary · BIG WHEELS

Travis saw some big wheels at the truck show.
Draw a line to match each word with the truck it describes.

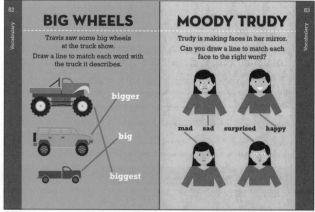

bigger
big
biggest

83 · MOODY TRUDY

Trudy is making faces in her mirror.
Can you draw a line to match each face to the right word?

mad · sad · surprised · happy

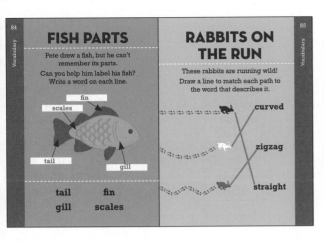

FISH PARTS

Pete drew a fish, but he can't remember its parts.

Can you help him label his fish? Write a word on each line.

fin
scales
tail
gill

tail   fin
gill   scales

RABBITS ON THE RUN

These rabbits are running wild! Draw a line to match each path to the word that describes it.

curved
zigzag
straight

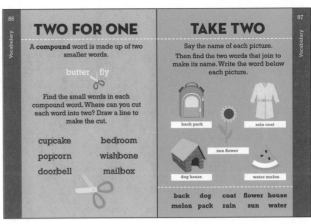

TWO FOR ONE

A **compound** word is made up of two smaller words.

butter | fly

Find the small words in each compound word. Where can you cut each word into two? Draw a line to make the cut.

cupcake   bedroom
popcorn   wishbone
doorbell   mailbox

TAKE TWO

Say the name of each picture. Then find the two words that join to make its name. Write the word below each picture.

back pack   rain coat
sun flower
dog house   water melon

back   dog   coat   flower   house
melon   pack   rain   sun   water

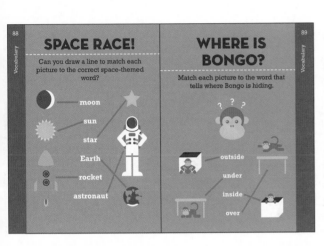

SPACE RACE!

Can you draw a line to match each picture to the correct space-themed word?

moon
sun
star
Earth
rocket
astronaut

WHERE IS BONGO?

Match each picture to the word that tells where Bongo is hiding.

outside
under
inside
over

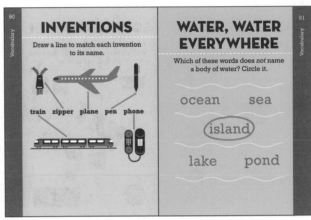

INVENTIONS

Draw a line to match each invention to its name.

train   zipper   plane   pen   phone

WATER, WATER EVERYWHERE

Which of these words does *not* name a body of water? Circle it.

ocean   sea
(island)
lake   pond

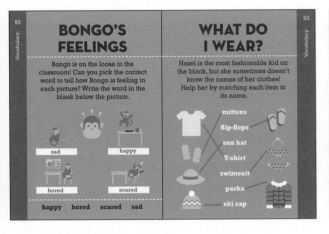

BONGO'S FEELINGS

Bongo is on the loose in the classroom! Can you pick the correct word to tell how Bongo is feeling in each picture? Write the word in the blank below the picture.

sad   happy
bored   scared

happy   bored   scared   sad

WHAT DO I WEAR?

Hazel is the most fashionable kid on the block, but she sometimes doesn't know the names of her clothes! Help her by matching each item to its name.

mittens
flip-flops
sun hat
T-shirt
swimsuit
parka
ski cap

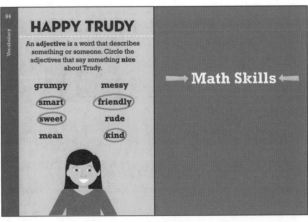

HAPPY TRUDY

An **adjective** is a word that describes something or someone. Circle the adjectives that say something **nice** about Trudy.

grumpy   messy
(smart)   (friendly)
(sweet)   rude
mean   (kind)

➡ **Math Skills** ⬅

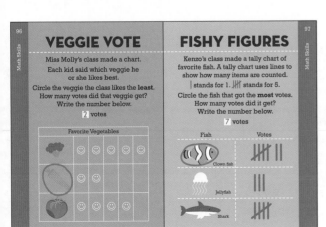

VEGGIE VOTE

Miss Molly's class made a chart.

Each kid said which veggie he or she likes best.

Circle the veggie the class likes the **least**. How many votes did that veggie get? Write the number below.

2 votes

Favorite Vegetables

FISHY FIGURES

Kenzo's class made a tally chart of favorite fish. A tally chart uses lines to show how many items are counted.

| stands for 1. ||||| stands for 5.

Circle the fish that got the **most** votes. How many votes did it get? Write the number below.

7 votes

Fish	Votes
Clown fish	|||| |||
Jellyfish	|||
Shark	||||	

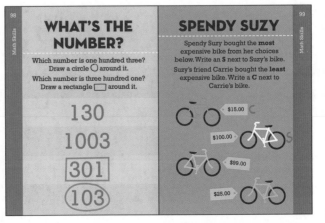

WHAT'S THE NUMBER?

Which number is one hundred three? Draw a circle ◯ around it.

Which number is three hundred one? Draw a rectangle ▭ around it.

130
1003
[301]
(103)

SPENDY SUZY

Spendy Suzy bought the **most** expensive bike from her choices below. Write an **S** next to Suzy's bike.

Suzy's friend Carrie bought the **least** expensive bike. Write a **C** next to Carrie's bike.

$15.00   C
$100.00   S
$99.00
$25.00

TREASURE CHEST

Priscilla the pirate found three treasure chests. Which one contains the **most** money? Circle it.

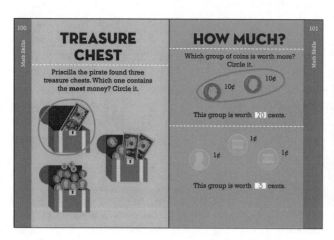

HOW MUCH?

Which group of coins is worth more? Circle it.

10¢   10¢

This group is worth `20` cents.

1¢

1¢   1¢

This group is worth `3` cents.

LICENSE PLATES

Alex and Amanda are playing a game on a family trip. The person who finds the highest number on a license plate wins.

This is the license plate Alex picked:

CALIFORNIA
4133

And this is the license plate Amanda picked:

PENNSYLVANIA
1999

Circle the winner.

Now circle the winner of this round:

Alex picked:
MARYLAND
2018

Amanda picked:
INDIANA
3009

Last round! Who won?

Alex picked:
UTAH
4991

Amanda picked:
MONTANA
4892

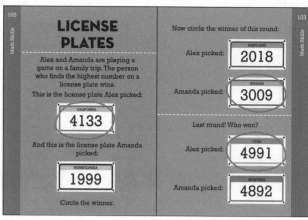

SPENDY SUZY II

Spendy Suzy is shopping for chairs. She decides to buy the **most** expensive one. Write an **S** next to Suzy's chair.

Suzy's friend Carrie bought the **least** expensive chair. Write a **C** next to Carrie's chair.

$147.99

$450.00   S

$200.00

$45.00   C

SQUARE SEARCH

How many squares do you see below? Make a check mark ✓ inside each one. Write the number here: `6`

TRI TRI AGAIN

How many triangles do you see below? Make a check mark inside each one. Write the number here: `7`

WHAT'S THE NUMBER? II

Which number is thirty-three? Make a circle ◯ around it.
Which number is three hundred thirty-three? Make a box ☐ around it.

30

333

33

3

QUACK ATTACK!

Draw a line to split the ducks in each box into two equal groups.

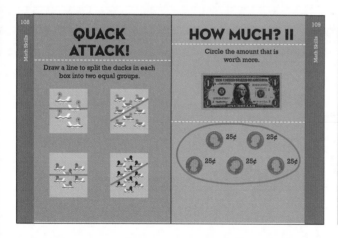

HOW MUCH? II

Circle the amount that is worth more.

THE UNITED STATES OF AMERICA
ONE DOLLAR

25¢   25¢
25¢   25¢   25¢

TALLY HO!

Mike's class made a tally chart to show their favorite ocean animals. Use the tally chart to answer the questions.

- How many children chose the dolphin? `5`
- Which animal got the **fewest** votes?
  `shark`
- Which animals got the **same** amount of votes?
  `dolphin`   `crab`

dolphin	🐬	丗
shark	🦈	IIII
seal	🦭	丗 IIII
crab	🦀	丗

MISSING PIECE

Kai put together his jigsaw puzzle but there's one piece missing. Which is it? Draw a line from the missing piece to the empty spot.

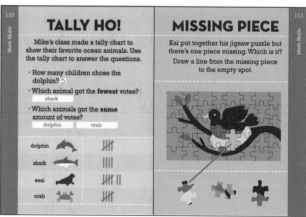

STUCK ON COINS!

Add **coin stickers** in the blanks so each group will add up to the amount shown.

◯ + ◯ ◯ = 7¢
5¢   1¢ 1¢

◯ + ◯ = 10¢
5¢   5¢

◯ + ◯ ◯ ◯ = 28¢
25¢   1¢ 1¢ 1¢

◯ ◯ + ◯ = 21¢
10¢ 10¢   1¢

◯ ◯ + ◯ = 15¢
5¢ 5¢   5¢

◯ + ◯ = 11¢
1¢   5¢ 5¢

◯ + ◯ ◯ = 12¢
1¢   10¢ 1¢

GREATER GROUPS

Count the things that go in each group.

Which group is **greater** than the other? Write this symbol **>** with the open part facing the **greater** group.

<   >

>

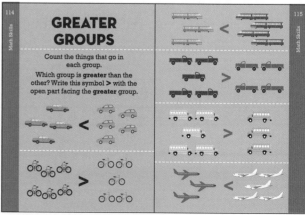

<   <

>

<

CHIP'S CHANGE

Chip has a pocket full of spare change. Can you help him put his coins in order from the smallest value to the largest?

Draw a line to show his path.

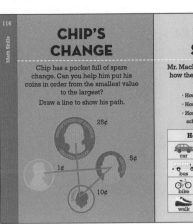

OFF TO SCHOOL

Mr. Mack's class made a chart to show how they get to school. Use the chart to answer the questions.

- How many students ride a bus? **4**
- How many students ride a bike? **2**
- How do most students get to school? **walk**

How We Travel to School

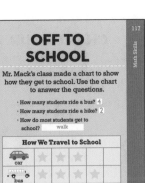

GREATER GROUPS II

Count the dinosaurs in each group. Which group is **greater** than the other? Write this symbol **>** with the open part facing the **greater** group.

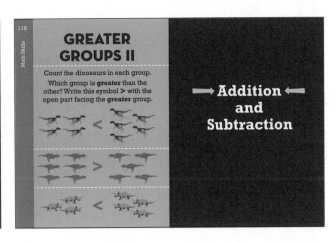

→ Addition ←
and
Subtraction

ONE MORE!

Max always wants one more! Count the toys in each group. Then draw a line to match it to the number that would be one more.

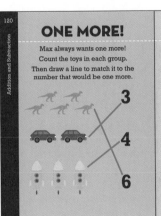

3

4

6

EVEN STEVEN

Steven wants to make his scale balance.

That means it must have the same amount of weight on both sides.

Draw in the number of weights that will make the scale balance.

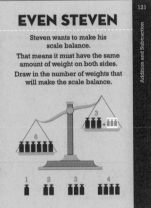

BERRY PICKING

All the muffins need to have **eight** cranberries.

Draw a line to each muffin to the amount of cranberries it still needs.

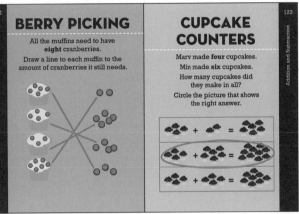

CUPCAKE COUNTERS

Marv made **four** cupcakes. Min made **six** cupcakes. How many cupcakes did they make in all?

Circle the picture that shows the right answer.

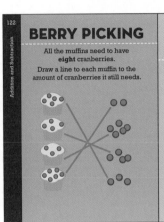

COOKIE COOKS

Ted and Ned made **ten** cookies. Each boy ate **one** cookie. How many cookies are left? Circle the picture that shows the right answer.

EVEN STEVEN II

Steven wants to make his scale balance.

That means it must have the same amount of weight on both sides.

Which two numbers will make the scale balance? Draw in the number of weights in the blanks.

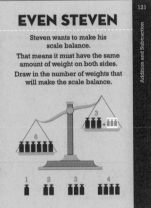

ONE TO NINE

Use your **number stickers** to fill in the answer for each number sentence. Each number from one to nine appears once.

10 − 3 = 7
8 − 5 = 3
6 − 2 = 4
9 − 4 = 5
4 − 2 = 2
2 − 1 = 1
10 − 2 = 8
9 − 3 = 6
10 − 1 = 9

PIZZA PARTY

Peyton loves pizza and he's having a party! His mom, dad, and two sisters are invited.

How many people will be at the party including Peyton? **5**

Which pizza is cut to serve each person **two slices**? Circle it.

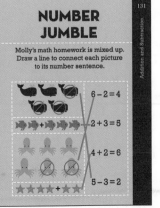

PARTY ANIMAL

All the animals were invited to play party games, except one. Solve each problem to find out who was left out. The letters above all the even number answers will spell the name of the animal.

Fill in the letters here to spell the name of the animal.
C H E E T A H

COOKIE COOKS II

Ruby and Maya made **eight** cookies. Each girl ate **two** cookies. How many cookies are left? Circle the picture that shows the right answer.

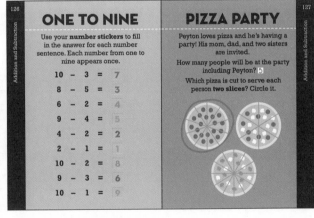

CUPCAKE COUNTERS II

Hannah made **three** cupcakes. Julia made **five** cupcakes. How many cupcakes did they make in all? Circle the picture that shows the right answer.

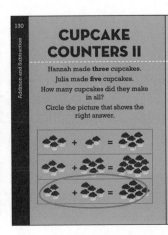

NUMBER JUMBLE

Molly's math homework is mixed up. Draw a line to connect each picture to its number sentence.

6 − 2 = 4

2 + 3 = 5

4 + 2 = 6

5 − 3 = 2

132

FRUITY FRAN

Fruity Fran ate three pineapples, two mangoes, and three bananas.

How many pieces of fruit did she eat in all? Complete the number sentence.

🍍🍍🍍 + 🥭🥭 + 🍌🍌🍌 = **8**

Kai ate much less. Complete this number sentence to see how much Kai ate.

🍍 + 🥭 + 🍌 = **5**

→ Shapes ←
and
Measurements

134

CHART YOUR SHAPES

Fill this chart with pictures of each shape and **number stickers**.

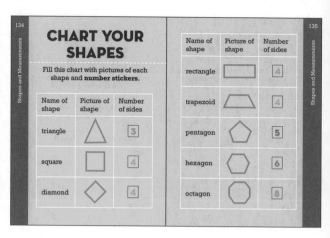

Name of shape	Picture of shape	Number of sides
triangle	△	3
square	□	4
diamond	◇	4

135

Name of shape	Picture of shape	Number of sides
rectangle	▭	4
trapezoid	⬯	4
pentagon	⬠	5
hexagon	⬡	6
octagon	⯃	8

136

TALENTED TRIANGLES

When triangles get together, they can make all sorts of shapes. See what you can make with your **triangle stickers**.

Can you make a square out of **2** triangles?

Can you make a rectangle out of **4** triangles?

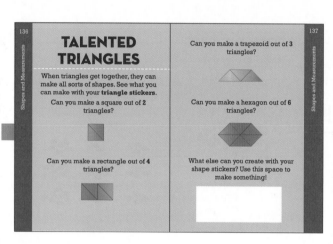

137

Can you make a trapezoid out of **3** triangles?

Can you make a hexagon out of **6** triangles?

What else can you create with your shape stickers? Use this space to make something!

138

BIG BUGS

Before the dinosaurs roamed, insects were huge! Some of their relatives are alive today.

Can you draw a line to match each insect to its size?

Hint: Compare the sizes of the pictures.

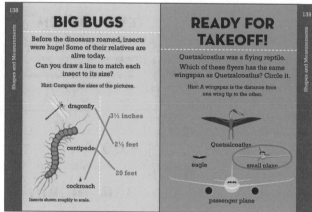

dragonfly — 3½ inches

centipede — 2½ feet

cockroach — 20 feet

Insects shown roughly to scale.

139

READY FOR TAKEOFF!

Quetzalcoatlus was a flying reptile. Which of these flyers has the same wingspan as Quetzalcoatlus? Circle it.

Hint: A wingspan is the distance from one wing tip to the other.

Quetzalcoatlus

eagle

small plane

passenger plane

140

SIZE ME UP

Spinosaurus was **one** school bus long.

Spinosaurus

How many school buses long was Seismosaurus? Write the number below.

Seismosaurus

3 school buses

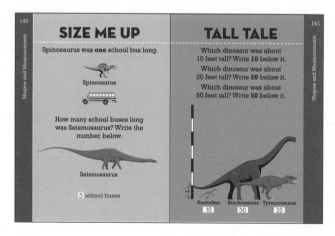

141

TALL TALE

Which dinosaur was about 10 feet tall? Write **10** below it.

Which dinosaur was about 20 feet tall? Write **20** below it.

Which dinosaur was about 50 feet tall? Write **50** below it.

Anatotitan **10**   Brachiosaurus **50**   Tyrannosaurus **20**

142

HEAVY WEIGHTS

Compare these dinosaurs. Can you draw a line to match each dinosaur to its weight?

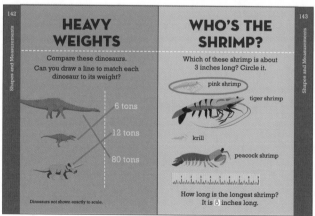

6 tons

12 tons

80 tons

Dinosaurs not shown exactly to scale.

143

WHO'S THE SHRIMP?

Which of these shrimp is about 3 inches long? Circle it.

pink shrimp

tiger shrimp

krill

peacock shrimp

How long is the longest shrimp? It is **8** inches long.

144

ORDER UP

Can you arrange these animals in order from smallest to largest? Write the correct order on the right. Start with the smallest on top.

cat — bee
mouse — mouse
horse — cat
whale — horse
bee — elephant
elephant — whale

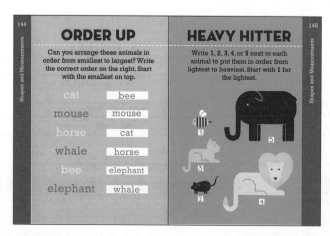

145

HEAVY HITTER

Write 1, 2, 3, 4, or 5 next to each animal to put them in order from lightest to heaviest. Start with **1** for the lightest.

1 bee
5 elephant
3 cat
2 mouse
4 lion

146

REPORT FOR DUTY!

It's up to you to give the weather report today!

Which thermometer shows the temperature for each picture? Draw a line to make each match.

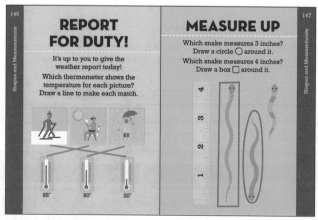

85°   60°   20°

147

MEASURE UP

Which snake measures 3 inches? Draw a circle ◯ around it.

Which snake measures 4 inches? Draw a box ☐ around it.

MEASURE UP II

Which animal measures
3.5 centimeters? Draw a circle ◯
around it.

Which animal measures
2 centimeters? Draw a box ☐
around it.

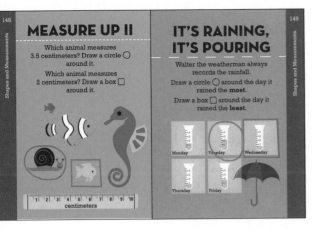

centimeters

IT'S RAINING, IT'S POURING

Walter the weatherman always
records the rainfall.

Draw a circle ◯ around the day it
rained the **most**.

Draw a box ☐ around the day it
rained the **least**.

Monday   Tuesday   Wednesday

Thursday   Friday

HOT STUFF!

Hal lives in the desert where it
can get really hot.

He records the temperature every day.

Write an **H** below the hottest day.
Write a **C** below the coolest day

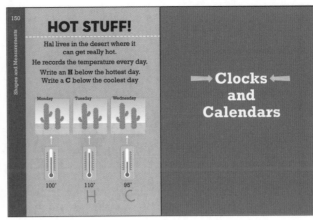

Monday   Tuesday   Wednesday

100°   110°   95°

→ **Clocks and Calendars** ←

WAKE UP, WALTER!

Walter needs to wake up at 6:10
in the morning.

Which alarm clock should he use?
Circle it.

DON'T BE LATE!

Ned delivers the newspaper.
He has to leave at 4:00 each morning.
Which clock shows the time he has
to leave? Circle the correct clock.

WAKE UP, WALTER II

Walter's phone rang at 10:30 last
night and woke him from a sound
sleep. Which clock shows the time
Walter woke up? Circle it.

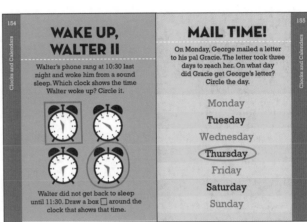

Walter did not get back to sleep
until 11:30. Draw a box ☐ around the
clock that shows that time.

MAIL TIME!

On Monday, George mailed a letter
to his pal Gracie. The letter took three
days to reach her. On what day
did Gracie get George's letter?
Circle the day.

Monday

Tuesday

Wednesday

(Thursday)

Friday

Saturday

Sunday

OUT OF ORDER!

Can you put these days in order
starting with Sunday? Write a **1, 2,
3, 4, 5, 6** or **7** next to each day to
put them in order.

Day	Order
Tuesday	3
Sunday	1
Friday	6
Monday	2
Saturday	7
Wednesday	4
Thursday	5

MISSING MONTH

Which month is missing. Circle it
below.

January

February

March

?

May

June

December   July
(April)   August

MAIL TIME! II

Gracie got George's letter on
Thursday and waited 12 days,
starting Thursday, to write back.
On which day did she write back?
Circle the day.

(Monday)

Tuesday

Wednesday

Thursday

Friday

Saturday

Sunday

HAPPY BIRTHDAY

Can you put these famous birthdays
in order? Write **1, 2, 3, 4,** or **5** next to
each date to put them in order.

Person	Order
Dr. Seuss: March 2	3
Oprah Winfrey: January 29	1
J. K. Rowling: July 31	5
Abraham Lincoln: February 12	2
William Shakespeare: April 23	4

HOLLY'S HOLIDAYS!

Can you help Holly put her holidays
in order? Which holiday comes
first in the year? Second? Third?
Write **1, 2,** or **3** next to each.

NEW YEAR'S DAY   1
FOURTH OF JULY   3
VALENTINE'S DAY   2

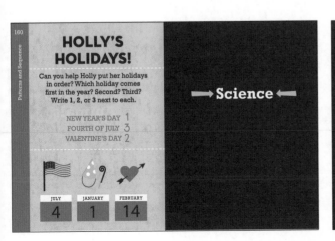

JULY   JANUARY   FEBRUARY
4   1   14

→ **Science** ←

ZIPPY ZEKE

Zeke wants to put these things in
order from slowest to fastest.
Can you help him?

Write **1, 2, 3,** or **4** next to each picture
to put them in order. Start with **1** for
the slowest.

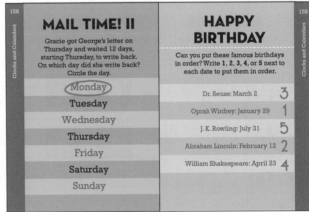

PLANET PUZZLER

Pete loves planets. Use the clues
to help Pete label his picture of the
planets.

• Mercury is next to the Sun.
• Mars is the farthest of these
  four planets from the Sun.
• Earth is next to Mars.
• Venus is next to Mercury.

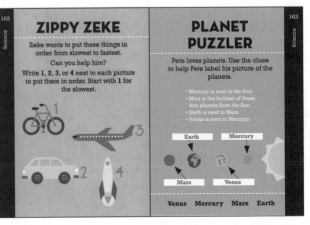

Earth   Mercury

Mars   Venus

Venus   Mercury   Mars   Earth

TIME TWISTER

All dinosaurs did not live at the same time. Use the chart to answer these questions.

Could Compsognathus attack Plateosaurus?
☐ yes ☒ no

Could Ankylosaurus whack Tyrannosaurus with its tail? ☒ yes ☐ no

Could Tyrannosaurus chase Apatosaurus?
☐ yes ☒ no

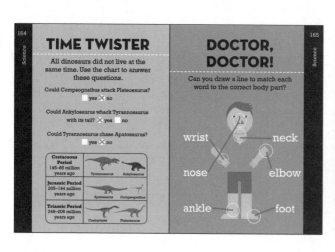

Cretaceous Period 145–65 million years ago	Tyrannosaurus	Ankylosaurus
Jurassic Period 205–144 million years ago	Apatosaurus	Compsognathus
Triassic Period 248–206 million years ago	Coelophysis	Plateosaurus

DOCTOR, DOCTOR!

Can you draw a line to match each word to the correct body part?

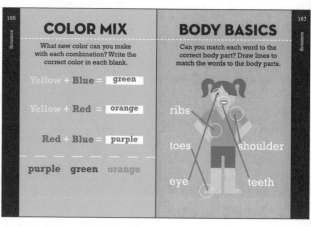

wrist   neck
nose   elbow
ankle   foot

COLOR MIX

What new color can you make with each combination? Write the correct color in each blank.

Yellow + Blue = green

Yellow + Red = orange

Red + Blue = purple

purple   green   orange

BODY BASICS

Can you match each word to the correct body part? Draw lines to match the words to the body parts.

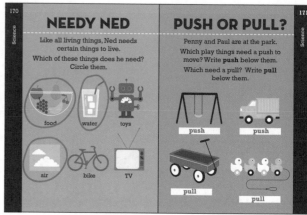

ribs
toes   shoulder
eye   teeth

STUCK ON YOU!

Molly has a magnet. Which things can she pick up with it? Circle them.

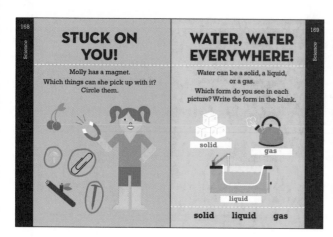

WATER, WATER EVERYWHERE!

Water can be a solid, a liquid, or a gas.

Which form do you see in each picture? Write the form in the blank.

solid
gas
liquid

solid   liquid   gas

NEEDY NED

Like all living things, Ned needs certain things to live.
Which of these things does he need? Circle them.

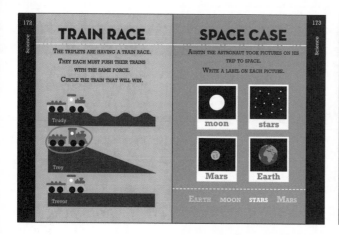

food   water   toys
air   bike   TV

PUSH OR PULL?

Penny and Paul are at the park. Which play things need a push to move? Write **push** below them.
Which need a pull? Write **pull** below them.

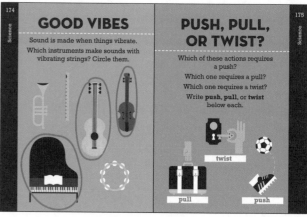

push   push
pull   pull

TRAIN RACE

THE TRIPLETS ARE HAVING A TRAIN RACE. THEY EACH MUST PUSH THEIR TRAINS WITH THE SAME FORCE. CIRCLE THE TRAIN THAT WILL WIN.

Trudy
Troy
Trevor

SPACE CASE

AUSTIN THE ASTRONAUT TOOK PICTURES ON HIS TRIP TO SPACE.
WRITE A LABEL ON EACH PICTURE.

moon   stars
Mars   Earth

EARTH   MOON   STARS   MARS

GOOD VIBES

Sound is made when things vibrate. Which instruments make sounds with vibrating strings? Circle them.

PUSH, PULL, OR TWIST?

Which of these actions requires a push?
Which one requires a pull?
Which one requires a twist?
Write **push**, **pull**, or **twist** below each.

twist
pull   push

SOLID SCIENCE

Which of the following pictures show only solids? Write an **S** below them.

S
S   S

GET ORGAN-IZED

Which two of these body organs do you need to digest your food? Draw a circle ◯ around the names.

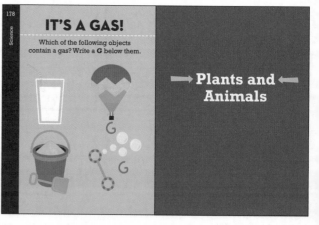

lungs   skin
stomach
intestines

Which organ helps you breathe? Draw a box ☐ around its name.

IT'S A GAS!

Which of the following objects contain a gas? Write a **G** below them.

G
G
G

→ Plants and ←
Animals

BACKBONE OR NOT?

A vertebrate is an animal with a backbone.

Which of these animals are vertebrates? Circle them.

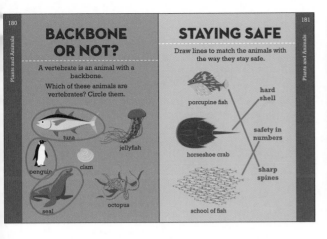

tuna
jellyfish
penguin
clam
seal
octopus

STAYING SAFE

Draw lines to match the animals with the way they stay safe.

porcupine fish — hard shell

safety in numbers

horseshoe crab — sharp spines

school of fish

NO BACKBONE!

An invertebrate is an animal without a backbone.

Which of these sea animals are invertebrates? Circle them.

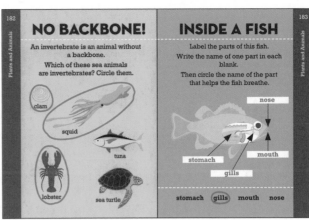

clam
squid
tuna
lobster
sea turtle

INSIDE A FISH

Label the parts of this fish.

Write the name of one part in each blank.

Then circle the name of the part that helps the fish breathe.

nose
stomach
mouth
gills

stomach gills mouth nose

COOL COLONIES

Cora Coral has a soft body and a hard outer skeleton. Cora and other corals live together in colonies. What do these colonies form? Draw a line from Cora Coral to the answer.

volcano
reef
cave

TEENY TINY

Tiny animal and plant-like organisms are at the bottom of the ocean food chain.

Can you draw a line to match each tiny living thing to its name?

krill
(a tiny shrimp)

water flea

diatom
(a tiny plant)

WHAT AM I?

I have no brain or bones.
I have no heart or eyes.
My body is made up of 95 percent water.
I am a predator, a good hunter.
What am I? Circle me.

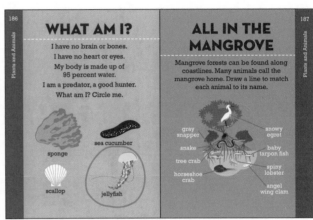

sponge
sea cucumber
scallop
jellyfish

ALL IN THE MANGROVE

Mangrove forests can be found along coastlines. Many animals call the mangrove home. Draw a line to match each animal to its name.

gray snapper
snake
tree crab
horseshoe crab
snowy egret
baby tarpon fish
spiny lobster
angel wing clam

DORA'S DOLPHIN

Dora drew a picture of a dolphin. Can you help her label its parts? Write the name of a part in each blank.

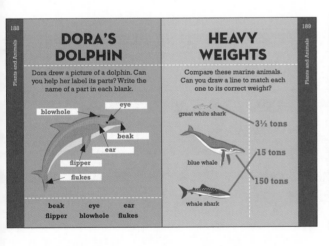

blowhole
eye
beak
ear
flipper
flukes

beak eye ear
flipper blowhole flukes

HEAVY WEIGHTS

Compare these marine animals. Can you draw a line to match each one to its correct weight?

great white shark
blue whale
whale shark

3½ tons
15 tons
150 tons

WHAT'S FOR DINNER?

A coral reef is made up of many thousands of tiny animals. Each one has a mouth surrounded by stingers. Coral animals cannot move.

Which of these could be a coral animal's dinner? Circle them.

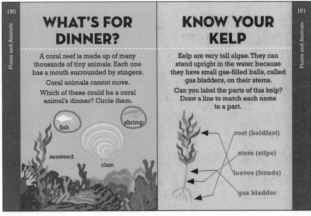

fish
shrimp
seaweed
clam

KNOW YOUR KELP

Kelp are very tall algae. They can stand upright in the water because they have small gas-filled balls, called gas bladders, on their stems.

Can you label the parts of this kelp? Draw a line to match each name to a part.

root (holdfast)
stem (stipe)
leaves (fronds)
gas bladder

A WHALE OF A TAIL

Lee went on a whale-watching trip. Help Lee write captions for his photos. Draw a line to match each photo to what the whale is doing.

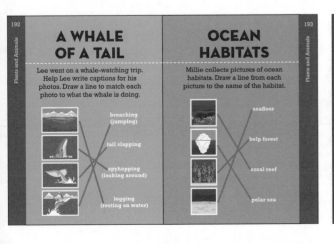

breaching (jumping)
tail slapping
spyhopping (looking around)
logging (resting on water)

OCEAN HABITATS

Millie collects pictures of ocean habitats. Draw a line from each picture to the name of the habitat.

seafloor
kelp forest
coral reef
polar sea

FIND THE PLANTS

Nate went on a nature walk and found some seeds. Which plants did they come from? Draw a line to match each seed to a plant.

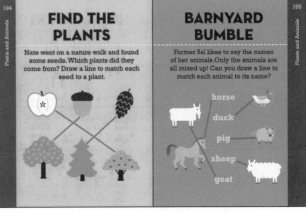

BARNYARD BUMBLE

Farmer Sal likes to say the names of her animals. Only the animals are all mixed up! Can you draw a line to match each animal to its name?

horse
duck
pig
sheep
goat

Answers

OUT OF AFRICA

Annie just got back from a trip to Africa. Fill in the blanks to spell the names of four animals she saw there.

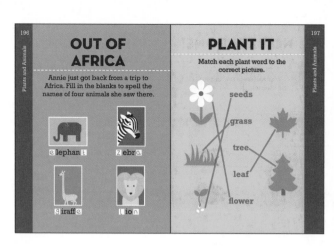

e lephan t.

z ebr a.

g iraffe

l io n

PLANT IT

Match each plant word to the correct picture.

seeds

grass

tree

leaf

flower

IT'S A STAGE

Here are some pictures of the life of a butterfly.

Write 1, 2, 3, or 4 next to each picture to put them in order. Start with 1 for the smallest.

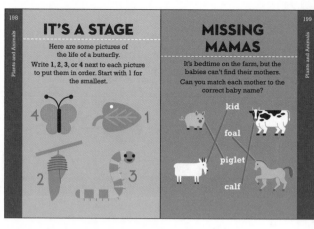

4   1

2   3

MISSING MAMAS

It's bedtime on the farm, but the babies can't find their mothers.

Can you match each mother to the correct baby name?

kid

foal

piglet

calf

HOME, SWEET HOME

Can you draw a line to match each animal to the place where it lives?

whale   toucan

rain forest   ocean   desert   tundra

polar bear   camel

BUG OFF!

Betsy goes buggy for bugs. Can you help her match the correct name to each bug? Draw a line to make each match.

beetle   fly   ant   dragonfly   bee

ALL MIXED UP

Sam saw lots of animals on his trip around the world, but he labeled his pictures wrong! Cross out Sam's labels and write the real animal name in the blank below each picture.

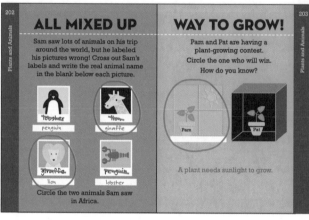

~~lobster~~   penguin

~~lion~~   giraffe

~~giraffe~~   lion

~~penguin~~   lobster

Circle the two animals Sam saw in Africa.

WAY TO GROW!

Pam and Pat are having a plant-growing contest.

Circle the one who will win.

How do you know?

Pam   Pat

A plant needs sunlight to grow.

WHICH CAME FIRST?

Draw lines to connect the mothers and the babies. Write a B next to the baby in each pair.

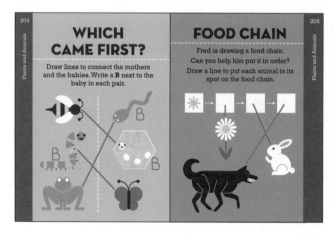

B

B   B

FOOD CHAIN

Fred is drawing a food chain. Can you help him put it in order? Draw a line to put each animal in its spot on the food chain.

EGG-CELLENT!

It's an animal egg hunt! Can you figure out which eggs belong to each animal? Draw a line to connect each animal to its eggs.

LIZARD LEAP!

Lizzie Lizard wants to go to the Lizard Lounge. She can only leap to pictures of reptiles.

Draw a line to show her path.

Lizard Lounge

Lizzie can move across, down, and diagonally.

POND PALS

Mi Won has a pond in her yard. Which of these plants and animals might you see there? Circle them.

HOME, SWEET HOME II

Can you draw a line to match each animal to the place where it lives?

goat   penguin

African grassland   steep mountains   cold tundra   forest

deer   giraffe

FEATHERS OR FUR?

Zed the zookeeper has mixed up his mammals and birds.

Can you sort them out for him?

Write an M next to the mammals.
Write a B next to the birds.

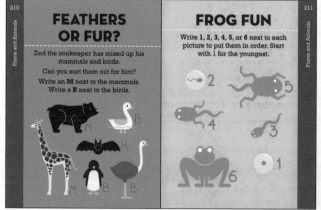

M   B

M   M

M   B

FROG FUN

Write 1, 2, 3, 4, 5, or 6 next to each picture to put them in order. Start with 1 for the youngest.

2   5

4   3

6   1

212 — GIVE ME SHELTER

Plants and Animals

These animals want to go home. Can you draw a line to match each animal to where it finds shelter?

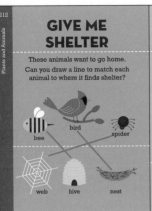

bee · bird · spider
web · hive · nest

213 — GIVE ME SHELTER II

Which two of these animals find shelter in a tree?
Which ones find shelter in a burrow? Draw lines to match the animals to their habitats.

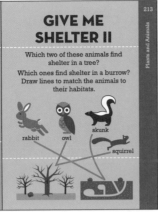

rabbit · owl · skunk · squirrel

214 — SEEDY STORY

Plants and Animals

Can you draw a line to match each seed to its parent plant?

215 — ICE IS NICE

Which two of these animals would camouflage (blend in) best on snow or ice? Draw a circle ◯ around them.

leopard · polar bear · arctic fox · bat

Which one would camouflage best at night? Draw a box ☐ around it.

216 — WILD THINGS!

Plants and Animals

Write a **W** next to the wild animals. Write an **F** next to the ones you'd find on a farm.

→ Earth and ← Weather

218 — RAIN OR SNOW?

Earth and Weather

Storm clouds are coming! Charlie's thermometer says the temperature is 14°F. Will it rain or snow? Circle one.

rain · **snow**

32°
14°

Hint: Water freezes when the temperature drops below 32°F.

219 — SKATE STORY

Earth and Weather

Skylar and Scotty want to ice-skate. But they have to wait for their ponds to freeze.

Circle the person who will wait longer.

Skylar · Scotty

220 — ICEBERG QUIZ

Earth and Weather

Icebergs float in the ocean. Is there more iceberg above the water surface or below? Check the box you think is right.

☑ Most is **under** the surface.
☐ Most is **above** the surface.

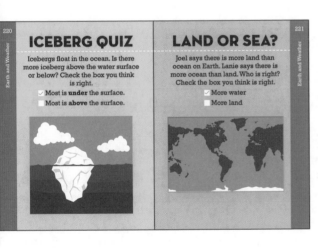

221 — LAND OR SEA?

Joel says there is more land than ocean on Earth. Lanie says there is more ocean than land. Who is right? Check the box you think is right.

☑ More water
☐ More land

222 — HOW'S THE WEATHER?

Earth and Weather

Draw a line to match each weather word to the correct picture.

rain
snow
wind
sunshine
cloud

223 — WHAT DO I WEAR?

Hazel is the most fashionable kid on the block. She doesn't always dress for the right season, however. Which clothes should Hazel wear in the summer? Write an **S** below them.

224 — WHAT DO I WEAR? II

Earth and Weather

Hazel is the most fashionable kid on the block. She doesn't always dress for the right season, however! Which items from her closet should she wear in the winter? Write a **W** by them.

225 — 'TIS THE SEASON

Joe likes taking pictures of his backyard. He takes a picture whenever the seasons change.

Write the name of each season below the picture.

winter · summer
spring · fall

fall · winter · spring · summer

226 — TOOL TIME

Earth and Weather

Tina uses different tools to learn about the weather.

Can you draw a line to match each tool to what it tells Tina?

temperature
wind direction
rainfall

227 — EARTH DAY

Earth and Weather

Ernest is making an Earth Day poster. Which pictures show ways to help the environment? Circle them.

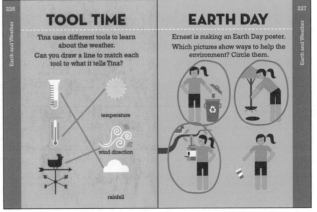

WATER WORKS

Inga is doing a project on the water cycle. Can you help her write the labels on her poster? Two have been done for you already.

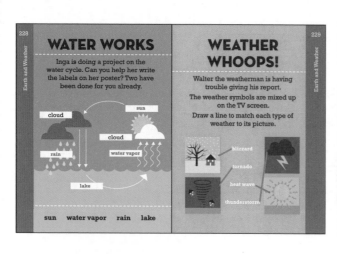

sun   water vapor   rain   lake

WEATHER WHOOPS!

Walter the weatherman is having trouble giving his report.

The weather symbols are mixed up on the TV screen.

Draw a line to match each type of weather to its picture.

blizzard
tornado
heat wave
thunderstorm

COLOR YOUR WORLD

Color all seven continents on this world map.

Color North America blue.
Color South America orange.

Color Africa yellow.
Color Europe red.
Color Asia purple.
Color Australia green.
Leave Antartica white.

WEATHER REPORT

What's the weather like where you live right now? Be a weather reporter and fill out the chart below!

Today's date is:

month   day   year

Check the boxes that describe the weather:

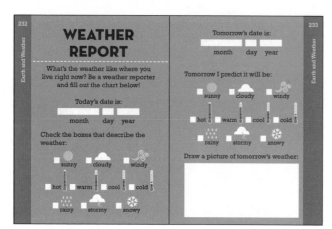

sunny   cloudy   windy
hot   warm   cool   cold
rainy   stormy   snowy

Tomorrow's date is:

month   day   year

Tomorrow I predict it will be:

sunny   cloudy   windy
hot   warm   cool   cold
rainy   stormy   snowy

Draw a picture of tomorrow's weather:

HOT LAVA

Laura loves volcanoes. She took pictures of this volcano when it erupted.

Write 1, 2, 3, or 4 next to each picture to put them in order from first to last.

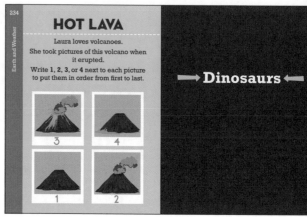

3   4
1   2

→ Dinosaurs ←

NAME GAME

Deinonychus was a dinosaur. Its name means "terrible claw." Which picture shows Deinonychus? Cirlce it.

SKELETON SEARCH

A vertebrate is an animal with a backbone. Think about what animals with backbones look like today.

Which of these ancient animals were vertebrates? Circle them.

Zalambdalestes   prehistoric jellyfish
Xiphactinus   Protoceratops

TREE TOPPER

These dinosaurs dined on different kinds of food.

Look at their body parts.

Which one could eat the leaves of tall trees? Circle it.

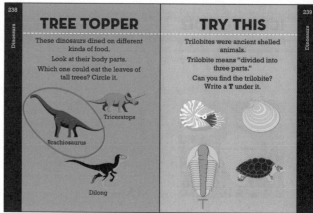

Triceratops
Brachiosaurus
Dilong

TRY THIS

Trilobites were ancient shelled animals.

Trilobite means "divided into three parts."

Can you find the trilobite? Write a T under it.

SO SPINELESS!

An invertebrate is an animal with no backbone.

Think about what animals with backbones look like. Which of these ancient animals did not have one? Circle them.

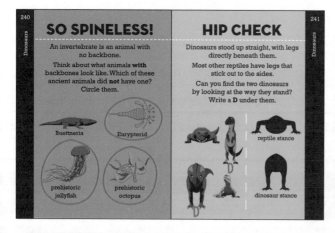

Buettneria   Eurypterid
prehistoric jellyfish   prehistoric octopus

HIP CHECK

Dinosaurs stood up straight, with legs directly beneath them.

Most other reptiles have legs that stick out to the sides.

Can you find the two dinosaurs by looking at the way they stand? Write a D under them.

reptile stance
dinosaur stance

EGGS-ACTLY!

All these animals lived in dinosaur times.

Can you draw a line to match each animal to its eggs?

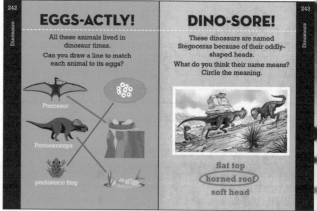

Pterosaur
Protoceratops
prehistoric frog

DINO-SORE!

These dinosaurs are named Stegoceras because of their oddly-shaped heads.

What do you think their name means? Circle the meaning.

flat top
horned roof
soft head

MEAT OR PLANTS

Meat-eaters have sharp teeth for tearing meat. Plant-eaters have mostly flat teeth for grinding plants.

Look at these dinosaur skulls.

Write an **M** below the meat-eaters.

Write a **P** below the plant-eaters.

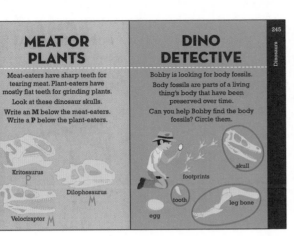

Kritosaurus — P
Dilophosaurus — M
Velociraptor — M

DINO DETECTIVE

Bobby is looking for body fossils. Body fossils are parts of a living thing's body that have been preserved over time.

Can you help Bobby find the body fossils? Circle them.

footprints, skull, tooth, egg, leg bone

DINO DETECTIVE II

Tracey is looking for trace fossils. Trace fossils are not part of an animal. They are fossils that show what a living thing was doing.

Can you help Tracey find the trace fossils? Circle them.

eggs, tooth, poop, footprint

MINI MAMMALS

Most of the mammals that lived at the same time as dinosaurs were no bigger than a small dog.

Which mammals lived with the dinosaurs? Circle them.

Smilodon (5 feet long)
Deltatheridium (6 inches long)
Zalambdalestes (6 inches long)
Repenomamus (3 feet long)

All lengths are approximate.

REPTILE REST

Reggie Reptile wants to cool off in the shade. He can only move to pictures of reptiles. Draw a line to show his path.

Hint: Most reptiles, other than dinosaurs, have legs that stick out to the sides.

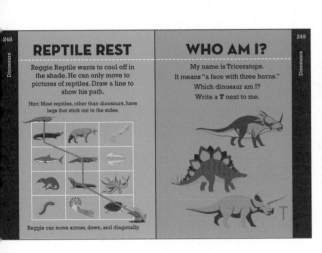

Reggie can move across, down, and diagonally.

WHO AM I?

My name is Triceratops. It means "a face with three horns."

Which dinosaur am I?

Write a **T** next to me.

T

EATING ON THE FLY

Pteranodon was a flying reptile that ate fish and possibly other animals. Pteranodon swallowed fish whole.

What bird today eats like this? Circle it.

robin, pelican, duck

WHAT'S MAI NAME?

This is Maiasaura.

The picture gives a clue about how it got its name.

What do you think this dinosaur's name means? Circle the meaning.

big-toothed lizard
curious lizard
good-mother lizard

DINO DINER

Anton is drawing a food chain. Can you help him put it in order? Draw a line to put each animal in its spot.

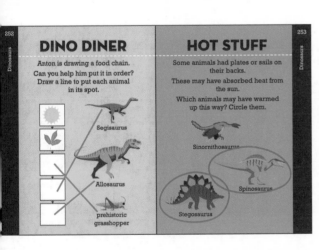

Segisaurus, Allosaurus, prehistoric grasshopper

HOT STUFF

Some animals had plates or sails on their backs. These may have absorbed heat from the sun.

Which animals may have warmed up this way? Circle them.

Sinornithosaurus, Stegosaurus, Spinosaurus

DINO DEFENSE

This is Ankylosaurus. Can you circle three body parts that it used to protect itself? Look at the list below for ideas.

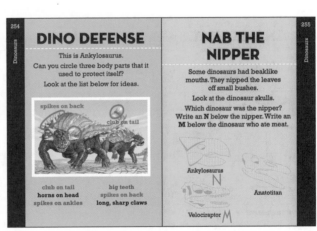

spikes on back, club on tail
club on tail, big teeth
horns on head, spikes on back
spikes on ankles, **long, sharp claws**

NAB THE NIPPER

Some dinosaurs had beaklike mouths. They nipped the leaves off small bushes.

Look at the dinosaur skulls. Which dinosaur was the nipper? Write an **N** below the nipper. Write an **M** below the dinosaur who ate meat.

Ankylosaurus — N
Anatotitan
Velociraptor — M

TRACE RACE

Pete the paleontologist is looking for a fossil skeleton. He can only move to pictures of **trace fossils**.

Can you draw a line to help him find his way?

Hint: Trace fossils show what a living thing was doing. They are not pieces of the actual animal.

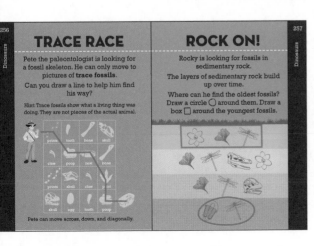

Pete can move across, down, and diagonally.

ROCK ON!

Rocky is looking for fossils in sedimentary rock. The layers of sedimentary rock build up over time.

Where can he find the oldest fossils? Draw a circle ◯ around them. Draw a box ☐ around the youngest fossils.

READY, SET, JET

While dinosaurs roamed the earth, other animals lived in the sea. Some moved by taking in water and squirting it out. This made them **jet** through the water.

Can you find the jetters below? Circle them.

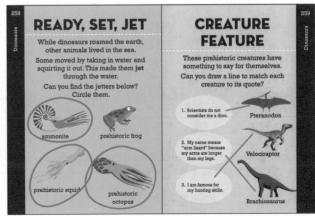

ammonite, prehistoric frog, prehistoric squid, prehistoric octopus

CREATURE FEATURE

These prehistoric creatures have something to say for themselves.

Can you draw a line to match each creature to its quote?

1. Scientists do not consider me a dino. — Pteranodon
2. My name means "arm lizard" because my arms are longer than my legs. — Velociraptor
3. I am famous for my hunting skills. — Brachiosaurus

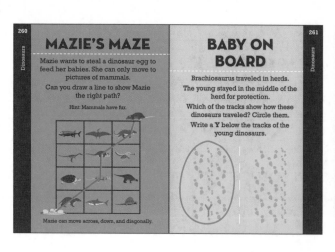

260 — MAZIE'S MAZE

Mazie wants to steal a dinosaur egg to feed her babies. She can only move to pictures of mammals.

Can you draw a line to show Mazie the right path?

Hint: Mammals have fur.

Mazie can move across, down, and diagonally.

261 — BABY ON BOARD

Brachiosaurus traveled in herds. The young stayed in the middle of the herd for protection.

Which of the tracks show how these dinosaurs traveled? Circle them.

Write a **Y** below the tracks of the young dinosaurs.

262 — WE ARE FAMILY

Gigantoraptor belongs to a family of birdlike dinosaurs.

Which dinosaur is the Gigantoraptor? Circle it.

263 — MINI MAMMALS

Mammals from dinosaur times were very small.

Which mammal did not live during the time of dinosaurs? Draw an **X** through it.

Circle the smallest mammal.

Mastodon (15 feet long)
Eomaia (5 inches long)
Megazostrodon (4 inches long)
Gobiconodon (18 inches long)
Animals not drawn to scale.

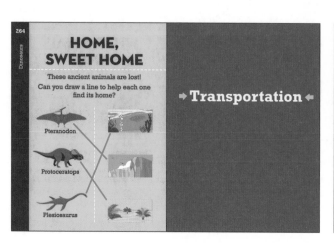

264 — HOME, SWEET HOME

These ancient animals are lost! Can you draw a line to help each one find its home?

Pteranodon

Protoceratops

Plesiosaurus

➤ Transportation ◄

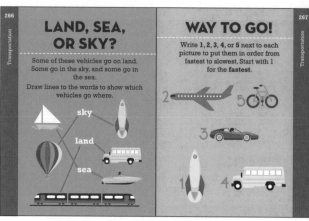

266 — LAND, SEA, OR SKY?

Some of these vehicles go on land. Some go in the sky, and some go in the sea.

Draw lines to the words to show which vehicles go where.

sky

land

sea

267 — WAY TO GO!

Write 1, 2, 3, 4, or 5 next to each picture to put them in order from fastest to slowest. Start with 1 for the **fastest**.

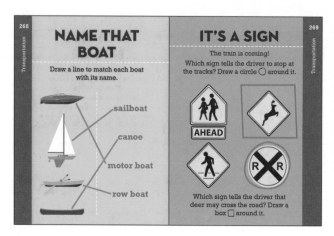

268 — NAME THAT BOAT

Draw a line to match each boat with its name.

sailboat

canoe

motor boat

row boat

269 — IT'S A SIGN

The train is coming! Which sign tells the driver to stop at the tracks? Draw a circle ◯ around it.

AHEAD

Which sign tells the driver that deer may cross the road? Draw a box ☐ around it.

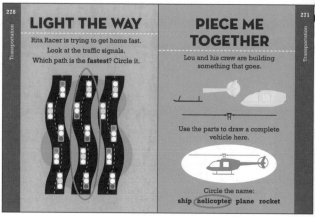

278 — LIGHT THE WAY

Rita Racer is trying to get home fast. Look at the traffic signals. Which path is the **fastest**? Circle it.

271 — PIECE ME TOGETHER

Lou and his crew are building something that goes.

Use the parts to draw a complete vehicle here.

Circle the name:

ship (helicopter) plane rocket

272 — SAFETY FIRST

Connect each picture to the way to make the person safer.

Two pictures have the same answer.

Wear a helmet

Sit down

Wear a seatbelt

➤ Games and Puzzles ◄

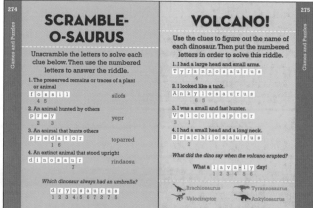

274 — SCRAMBLE-O-SAURUS

Unscramble the letters to solve each clue below. Then use the numbered letters to answer the riddle.

1. The preserved remains or traces of a plant or animal
f o s s i l   silofs
  4 5

2. An animal hunted by others
p r e y   yepr
2 3

3. An animal that hunts others
p r e d a t o r   toparred
  1 6

4. An extinct animal that stood upright
d i n o s a u r   rindaosu
       7

Which dinosaur always had an umbrella?

d r y o s a u r u s
1 2 3 4 5 6 7 2 7 5

275 — VOLCANO!

Use the clues to figure out the name of each dinosaur. Then put the numbered letters in order to solve this riddle.

1. I had a large head and small arms.
T y r a n n o s a u r u s
       4

2. I looked like a tank.
A n k y l o s a u r u s
      6 5

3. I was a small and fast hunter.
V e l o c i r a p t o r

4. I had a small head and a long neck.
B r a c h i o s a u r u s
    2

What did the dino say when the volcano erupted?

What a l a v a l y day!
     1 2 3 4 5 6

Brachiosaurus   Tyrannosaurus
Velociraptor   Ankylosaurus

GO FISH!

In this game, the person with the most pairs wins.

Who will win this round? Circle the winner.

Jack's cards

Jill's cards

Jack and Jill are playing another round, and this time, you're playing!

Jack's cards

Jill's cards

Circle the card you need to win.

Your cards

OCEAN PUZZLER

Unscramble the letters to solve each clue below. Then use the numbered letters to answer the riddle.

1. A movement of ocean water that reaches land.
w a v e   vewa
   3 4

2. This ocean animal is a mammal.
d o l p h i n   poldinh
     8 2 5

3. These tiny animals have hard skeletons that can form a reef.
c o r a l s   olacrs
7 9   1 6

Why are fish so smart?

Because they

l i v e i n s c h o o l s
1 2 3 4 2 5 6 7 8 9 9 9 1 6

TERMITE TRIP

Ted the termite wants to get to the house. He can only crawl on pictures of words that begin with t. Can draw a line to you help him find the path?

He can only go down or across.

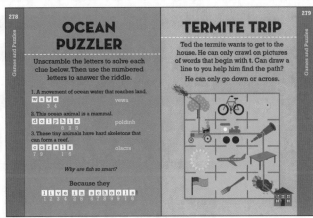

WORD PUZZLES

Paula has some puzzle pieces.

Can you make 9 words with her pieces? Write them below.

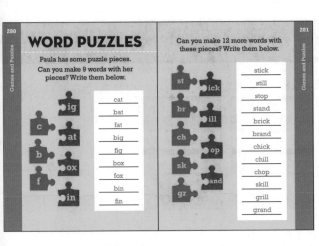

cat
bat
fat
big
fig
box
fox
bin
fin

Can you make 12 more words with these pieces? Write them below.

stick
still
stop
stand
brick
brand
chick
chill
chop
skill
grill
grand

MOVE IT

Can you find the three things in a row that do not belong with the rest?

You can go across or down. Circle them.

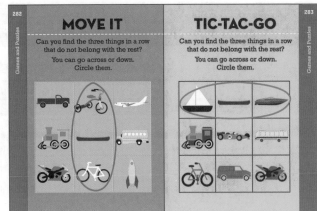

TIC-TAC-GO

Can you find the three things in a row that do not belong with the rest?

You can go across or down. Circle them.

BUGGY BUSINESS

Can you circle the two ladybugs that are exactly the same?

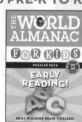

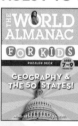
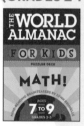
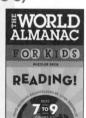